Ask And You
Shall Marry

Copyright © 2015 by Marricke Kofi Gane

ASK AND YOU SHALL MARRY

By Marricke Kofi Gane

ISBN: 978-1-909326-29-3

Published by MarrickeGanePublishing

Distributed by Amazon

Ask And You Shall Marry

A Diary Of 303 Questions
To Choose And Ask From
Before Marriage

By Marricke Kofi GANE

Contents

DEDICATION

This book is dedicated to Otzara, Chazona and Asher.
You are products of God's perfect intention for marriage.
May you all remain seeds of excellence in the hands of God.

Introduction

This book contains a diary of 303 questions from which to choose, ask and gain a better understanding of the person and journey of marriage you are about to embark on.

People make the argument that you can never know someone completely before marriage – some even go as far as saying it is not possible in a lifetime. I did not write this book to prove or disprove any of that.

What I do assert however, is that choosing and asking the right kind of questions before marriage can go a long way to prevent a lot of unnecessary surprises during marriage. It can also bring to fore, certain hitherto unexpressed expectations from both parties which would otherwise have crept unnoticed into the relationship, causing problems later. There are some things you need to discover about your partner in marriage – there are others you need to be sure about before you marry them.

If you asked the necessary questions and received the answers prior to marriage, then it is expected that you will assess your relationship – informed. Choosing to proceed to marriage, would suggest that you are making an informed choice which you hope will lead to a successful union. I submit that going through this process is also an act of love, in that you made the effort to ask the necessary questions in order to protect yourself and your future spouse from the consequences of selective ignorance.

This book is not a theoretical volume on relationship

psychology, but rather, it is a simple, no-nonsense book of questions that will help you better understand, appreciate and embrace what exactly it is you are about to get yourself into where marriage is concerned. Its authority is based on the Christian Bible, even though for the purposes of allowing a flow in the writing, I have created a separate reference section at the back that lists all the necessary Bible verses that have inspired its various sections.

Before you proceed, I wish to point out a few things I believe are reasonable to bear in mind when attempting to apply the contents of this book, practically:

- ✓ DON'T ATTEMPT TO ASK ALL 303 QUESTIONS in this book. Be realistic – it is a diary of questions – don't expect to ask them all.

- ✓ Not every question in this book is to be asked exactly the way it is written here. You need a bit of tact and an understanding of your partner's temperament in order to decide when and how to phrase the questions.

- ✓ Not all the questions in this book need be asked face to face, some can be answered from observation. The only caveat here is – be careful your mind and heart are not too clouded with strong emotions, else you run the risk of seeing or hearing the answers you want. I suggest that if you are relying on observation, don't assume your assessments are 100% correct – corroborate your observations. Remember, it is your life and you do not want to blame yourself in the future for making preventable but wrong judgements.

✓ Be aware that you may not get all the right answers from your partner – everybody likes to keep some things to their selves. What you should reasonably do however, is to figure out what matters most to you, choose and ask the questions pertaining to it. This should not be too difficult since you know yourself better than anybody else. For example, if it is crucially important for you not to be separated from your spouse for too long a time, then ask the questions about travelling that may arise relating to career, studying and the like.

✓ You must be ready to answer these questions yourself. It is only fair that if you ask these questions of your partner, you are willing to answer them too. It is most likely that any unwillingness on your part to answer these same questions will become a hindrance to you getting the answers that are important to you. In my view, your willingness to respond to these same questions is a small price to pay for the opportunity to get answers that can make the difference between a life time of pain or one of happiness in marriage.

    ✓   Asking and answering these questions openly and honestly will help to build trust and thereby lessen some of the possible shocks in marriage caused by a sense of betrayal. It could happen when something comes to light later in marriage that should have been disclosed to you prior. Your partner may have genuinely forgotten to tell you everything. For this reason, you owe it to yourself to ask at least some questions prior to marriage.

    ✓   This material can be used as a marriage counselling resource or simply shared by a couple intending to marry. It is useful resource to shape the quality and content of conversations had prior to marriage. It is structured in a manner that helps you agree on some areas of interaction before marriage. I can assure you that most of the issues covered in the book will arise in the future.

    ✓   There is a need to be honest with yourself about why you want your questions answered. Before using this book, you should decide that your intentions are not to find out about your partner in order to use it against them now or in the future. This will be a sure way of destroying your own relationship – it will not inspire any kind of trust.

✓   At times, expect the answer to one question to conflict with another – use this as an opportunity to seek clarification on the topic, thereby, dispelling doubts.

I hope you enjoy using this book and I pray it makes the marriage journey for you better.

Marricke Kofi Gane
Author

I

Personal & Individual Life

This section generally covers questions that will help you get a dual insight into (i) the peculiar attributes of your partner and (ii) what they also consider peculiar about you. In this section, the answers to the questions should hopefully begin to create a clearer picture of what makes them uniquely individual – and what you find may not all be exciting. It's an attempt to understand as much of their uniqueness as possible, in order to satisfy yourself, whether or not their individuality is one you are, or can become compatibly with.

1. *What is it about me that first attracted you to me?*

   Your partner's initial attraction to you is likely to be the most intuitively honest one. Find out what it is. It may serve as a useful comparison to other reasons given in the future after the mesmerizing spell of romance wears off.

2. *If you had the chance to change something about me, what would it be?*

   Don't take "nothing" for an answer. Insist that your partner is not too modest about their answer. If they are forthcoming, the answers are likely to give you a glimpse of what it is about yourself you need to make an effort to work on, to increase the chances of your relationship being successful.

3. *If nothing ever changes about me, would you still be happy marrying me for a lifetime?*

   This is a crucial test because most people subconsciously enter into a long term relationship with the hope that some things will change about their partner. This can become a serious problem when the change does not take place as hoped for.

4. *Where would you like to see your life in 5 years' time if I was not in the picture?*

   It's a good thing to know that you are on a bus that's heading in the direction you are happy with. It won't always be the case but at least it is important to know and determine whether your journeys are too wide apart or not. Perhaps you should find it interesting enough to ask "why" if very early in the relationship, your partner is prepared to alter their entire journey just for you to come on board.

5. *What is the one thing you are doing now, that if you were to stop doing in marriage, will make you feel you've lost a big part of yourself?*

Whatever the answer to this, it should be something that your partner treasures because of its importance to them. Guard this dearly and never use it as a weapon of manipulation against them.

6. *What is the one thing about yourself you would have loved to change if you had the chance?*

You should consider whether or not you can realistically help them make the change. If you can, they will greatly appreciate it, because you would have added value to them.

7. *What is the greatest achievement you are aspiring to in life, if everything was to work according to plan?*

It does not only indicate ambition, it also highlights at what point in their life, fulfilment can be assumed to have been attained. But until they get there, this knowledge will help you understand some of the choices they make and why they make it.

8.   *What are the five big things that irritate you the most?*

These are like red flags, some of which you may not be able to avoid, but knowing what they are will stop you from making some big blunders. Whatever these are, you need to consciously try to avoid them until it becomes second nature to you.

9.   *What are the five big things that excite or make you happy?*

These are some of the golden keys to making your partner happy. If you know and apply them appropriately, you can get it right with them more often than you get it wrong. Do remember though, that human beings grow and change over time, so this topic might require re-visiting from time to time.

10. *What are three habits you have that not many people know about?*

Since habits take years to develop, it makes sense to come to terms with two truths: (i) you cannot change them any time soon and so (ii) you will have to live with them at some point. Preparing to encounter them will most definitely lessen the likely negative impact, if any on you.

11. *Are there any past or current financial problems you have that I should know about?*

This information is vital because of the importance of money in people's lives. Therefore, this is one question to which you should try and get an honest response. If they have financial problems like gambling debts If they are financial problems like gambling debts or unpaid loans, then you need to know the details because by marrying the person, you become partly responsible for their debts. The conversation can also give you an insight into whether the problem is chronic or one-off and how responsible the person has been in dealing with money matters.

12. *Do you currently or have in the past had any health issues that I should know about?*

This is one of those things you will hardly know except you ask. Looking healthy is quite different from being healthy – it cannot be determined by mere observation, so you need to ask. By the way, if a health condition exists, you need to find out what the long-term prognosis is and what is currently being done about it. It may also be helpful to find out if it is hereditary or not. Hopefully, your partner is making every effort to pursue a healthy life style.

13. *What is the best way you like to be engaged when you are*
    angry about something?

When most people are angry, reason flies out of the window
and emotions take over. So it is good to know how a person
wants to be treated when this happens. The partner who is
not angry might react in a manner that only exacerbates the
situation, so knowing how they want to be treated can help
to defuse the situation.

14. *How do you usually deal with disappointments and*
    failures?

Again, this is very personal and can vary from person to
person. Your focus, however, should be on how to coax your
partner out of the hole of disappointment. The longer they
stay in it, the greater the chances it can turn into something
close to depression.

15. *How good are your housekeeping skills, personal and home*
    hygiene?

This question is an important one because some people do
not place a great deal of value on domestic and personal
hygiene due to their upbringing. Because you may value
these things, it does not automatically mean it is the same for
your partner and vice versa.

16. *What would you say is proof of your ability to be committed (or what have you been most committed to, to date)?*

Even a glimpse is good enough. Commitment is the mainframe of any good relationship. If it has not been demonstrated even at a basic level such as committing to a regular job or in other ways, it is going to be hard for the person to start it for the very first time in marriage. It is not a guarantee that if they have shown commitment in the past, they will to you – but it is better than walking in the dark altogether.

17. *What is your definition of responsibility and how do you expect it to be demonstrated?*

You may be surprised how people view responsibility, hence the need to talk about it together to arrive at a common understanding so there will be no unpleasant surprises later on.

18. *Can you paint a picture to me of where you eventually want to arrive in life?*

Truth be told, if your partner has no picture in their mind about where they expect to end up in life or if they cannot describe it, then it is hardly likely that they will know when they have arrived at their destination or are on track for getting there. This can result in a feeling of un-fulfilment and low self- morale, especially during trying times. When your partner has a vision and is able to articulate it, you are in a better position to determine how to help them get there.

19. *What are you naturally good at?*

Knowing a person's natural talent and capabilities will help you fathom why they focus on certain activities and behave the way they do. On the other hand, if they are not pursuing the things they are naturally outstanding at, it should be a signal to you they will soon start feeling unfulfilled. You can help to channel them in the right direction based on their obvious strengths.

20. *What are your top three hobbies and how regularly do you engage in them?*

Here is an indication of whether or not your partner has some balance in their life. Having a hobby is one thing – consciously engaging in it for its benefits is quite another. It will also indicate how the person will want to spend their free time.

21. *What are some of your favourite indulgences?*

In any relationship, the obvious aim is to try and be the one that gets most things right with your partner. This includes knowing what they like best and can pertain to food, drink, movies, type of music and such things.

22. *How do you get motivated or what drives you?*

Some people are simply self-motivated. Others need to be handed a bit of spark. From time to time, even those who are naturally self-motivated also need a boosting spark to move on. Do you know what it is for your partner? Can you provide it?

23. *Who is your role model or mentor?*

To make us better persons we all need someone to look up to as our role model. This can come in many forms and not necessarily by a physical presence. Any man or woman who has no role model or is not regularly inspired by anyone is an accident waiting to happen. Worse of all, by not having a mentor or a role model, he or she is likely to become his own god and accountable only to themselves.

24. *How do you naturally prefer to engage with life: treat it seriously, go with the flow or take it a day at a time?*

A lot of how your partner sees life has most likely been formed from how they were raised and the environment in which they grew up, as well as their natural disposition. You can always make that connection if you look close enough. There is little you can do to change this, but it gives you a gauge on their inclined response to life's issues.

25. *What has been your greatest regret in life to date?*

The answer to this question gives you an idea what paths your partner is most eager to steer clear off and inadvertently what paths you should try as much as possible not to lead them onto throughout your journey together.

26. *What has been your best achievement in life to date?*

Hopefully, this should strengthen what you already know about their dreams and where your partner is headed in life, generally.

27. *Who are your closest friends?*

Have you ever heard the expression, "show me your friends and I will show you your character?" Well, knowing your partner's friends will give you some insight into the influence on their their life.

28. *Do you consider "gratitude" as courteous or a requisite life principle?*

A grateful person is most likely to be a humble and appreciative individual with a realisation that they have a need for others. It is also very hard to look down on someone to whom you are grateful. A grateful person is also more likely to be kind and less suspicious of others.

29. *In what circumstance have you had to demonstrate the highest level of responsibility to date?*

Marriage demands maturity and a strong sense of responsibility. While being responsible in a given situation does not necessarily guarantee a repeat performance in marriage, at least it will demonstrate a tendency in this direction. The response to this question might be the best gauge you have for judging the matter. Look out for tendencies to "get things done" irrespective.

30. *What are your views about violence in a relationship?*

Spousal abuse is much too common these days, so any indications that your partner has a tendency to be violent should be taken seriously. While you cannot ask them directly if they are given to violence, body language and verbal inclinations can give you some clues as to their inert dispositions. A smart approach would also be to bring up for discussion a spousal abuse case in the news or in social circles and ask what they think about it.

31. *Have you ever been involved in any form of criminal activities?*

You certainly do not want to be associated with a person who is a habitual lawbreaker or who has committed crimes that are likely to be uncovered or convicted later in your relationship. Why do you need to know? After marriage, you will share equally in their identity, criminal or otherwise – irrespective of whether you actually participated in the wrongdoing or not.

32. Are you a member of any group publicly considered violent, terrorist or fanatic?

The underlying reason people align themselves to groups, movements or associations is because such entities stand for what they believe in. Knowing what these organisations stand for publicly or secretly is very likely what your partner stands for too even if they haven't been open about it. Are they good ideals?

33. How do you generally go about resolving conflict?

Conflicts are a natural part of any relationship and must be resolved if you wish the relationship to remain healthy. They shouldn't be happening – but they can happen. People have different approaches to conflict resolution- some prefer to delay action, tackle it immediately or leave it altogether. Knowing each other's preference for conflict resolution helps you formulate a strategy that works for you both. I was taught this principle early, that conflicts involve two persons at least – if you decide consciously not to partake of it, you weaken the chances of the conflict happening.

34. *What is your personal code on dressing and is there a certain manner you would best prefer that I dress?*

Both of you cannot expect to change each other's dress style. Knowing what manner of dressing each other is comfortable with and what is considered offensive can help you complement each other's style. Don't forget dressing plays an important role in physical attraction.

35. *In order of importance, how would you rank the following - family, work, religion or spirituality, social engagements and personal goals?*

This is a challenging question, but certainly one that forces your partner to identify their priorities. Over time, it is possible to match their answer with how you see them living their daily life.

36. *What is your greatest fear?*

Fear is natural; everyone has one or more things that they fear. It may well be your partner's area of greatest fear is an area you possess strength in and so, can complement them.

37. *Do you know how to cook – and how well?*

Some may consider this question unnecessary or think it should only apply to women. But a man does need some culinary skills too, no matter how minimal, as these may come in handy when the woman is ill or is in some other way incapacitated. But beyond all that, cooking for oneself could showcase a person as particular about their health. Whatever the reason, this is a good question for discussion.

38. *Where do you see yourself living in the next five to ten years?*

I have personally seen a decision around geographical location destroy an otherwise wonderful relationship. If at any time during courtship you're living in different geographical locations, where you will live together after marriage must be frankly discussed and mutually agreed on. Distance, does have the power to expose either of you to other "involvements"

39. *Are you liberal or frugal when it comes to spending money?*

Neither is bad. The value of liberality is in what money is spent on. The value of frugality is in what is sacrificed in the practice of that frugality. If you share differing views in this matter, then you need to find a creative way around the use of money.

40. *How important is it for you to make a lot of money?*

Ambition is good, but not when it is directed solely at making money. If money is their only ambition, there is a likelihood morality will be sacrificed to go after money. Desiring to be rich as an end in itself may encourage them to embrace any means to arrive at this end. This is not a healthy approach to achieving financial stability.

41. Do you function better with quietness around you or you draw energy from background activity?

Again, personalities differ based on natural inclination as well as social conditioning. Some people function best in solitude others thrive on the hustle and bustle of life around them. Whatever the preferred style, knowing it should help you to both respect and support each to function optimally.

42. Are you a morning or night person?

Again, the answers here come in handy in supporting each other and useful in very practical circumstances such as determining sleeping shifts between the two of you when babies are born or when you both operate a home business that requires operating day and night.

43. What makes you "tick?"

At some point, we all get distracted from being our optimal selves, sometimes due to unexpected problems, work, health and others. It helps when you, the closest to your partner, are able to both recognize when they are at their lowest and exactly what to do to get them back on track – fast.

44. *What are your greatest weaknesses?*

We all have weaknesses. It is a part of being human and so no modesty is needed about this. Telling all the truth here demands trust, but more importantly, this knowledge can help both of you to support each other in your different areas of weakness and strengthen the bond between you both.

45. *Are you generally open-minded and open to new ways of doing things?*

This question somewhat tests a bit of your partner's open-ness to creativity – and it could very well be creativity in all spheres, even intimacy, but not limited to it. It opens up for discussion, whether or not they have a tendency to be stuck with only what they know or are willing to continually evolve their learning and therefore their experiences, their engage-ment with life and insights.

46. *What is your favourite genre of music and books?*

The kind of music and lyrics one listens to often reflects their soul or inner self – deep thinking, calm or rowdy and loud. The same could be said of books. The content of music and reading they spend their time on can indicate areas of per-sonal aspiration and need they require fulfilment in.

2

Spirituality

Every human is made up of body, spirit and soul. It would be an incomplete assessment of your partner's suitability if you sought to understand their physical, mental and emotional states, but not their spiritual. The spiritual state of a person will always affect their two other states and vice versa. This section is written to help you not only assess their current spiritual state but also understand how it is likely to evolve over time, including in marriage. It will also highlight what their spiritual foundations are and where you two are likely to experience spiritual compatibilities and conflicts (if any). I have used the assumption there will be a good number of spiritual persons of the Christian faith (as it is my practicing faith) who will be looking to marry equally spiritual partners.

1. *What religious faith do you believe in and practice?*

    A person's spirituality and faith usually means a lot to them BUT you should never assume you know your partner's answer to this question until you have asked. The fact that you see your partner in church every Sunday for example, does not automatically mean they are followers of Christ. I don't mean to be cynical, but what if they are only there to find a good wife/husband?

2. *Do you share in the ideologies of other religious faiths you do not practice?*

    This is really not meant for you to be suspicious about your partner's religious commitment because people sometimes share the ideologies espoused by another faith. This is alright. However, if the ideologies of whatever other faith they believe in are the main and core ideologies of that faith, then you shouldn't be too surprised if they later decide to align fully with that other faith.

3. *What is the one temptation you will honestly find difficult to resist on your own?*

    This demands real honesty, and if your partner is truthful answering this, it will empower you to help them manage such temptations. It could help your discretion about when, where, what and who to leave them with. Nevertheless, this should not mean the imposition of various kinds of restrictions on your partner's freedom in the name of protecting them.

4. *Have you been part of any secret society and if so, will you still be after we marry?*

Until you ask, the idea will be to keep it exactly what it is – a secret. If your partner is a member of any such group that you are uncomfortable about, then you need to be certain as to whether or not they intend to continue or give up membership. If they're out of it, have they severed all connections? If they're still in it, be convinced that their membership poses no threat whatsoever to you.

5. *Have you made any secret or open vows or covenants with anyone, groups or associations and if so, do you still keep those vows and covenants?*

Vows are powerful binders. If your partner has entered any vows prior to your relationship, then understand, that vows simply don't vanish because they have stopped talking to someone, or stopped participating in a group's activities. If those prior vows are not revoked, they may very well conflict with your marital vows and cause you problems in marriage. Seek spiritual advice.

6. *Do you harbour any religious prejudices?*

   If they do and depending on what they are, such negative feelings have the potential to grow into stronger emotions such as hatred - which could be dangerous. Again, this will depend on the nature of the prejudice. It may as well be too trivial to develop into a strong emotional driver.'

7. *Has a topic or a religious practice ever been a reason for a problem in a previous relationship?*

   Knowing the nature of such past conflicts is useful to pre-empt which areas of your partner's spiritual pillars must not cross paths with your relationship or personal priorities.

8. *Do you believe in God or Evolution?*

   Well, this is by far one of the most fundamental questions about anything religious you both have to grapple with. You will both need to be clear about it. If your beliefs differ on this, it means your spiritual paths differ. From that point onwards, the real question that needs to be asked (although it is likely not to be) is: who will eventually convert who?

9. *Which God do you believe in and what are His attributes?*

   God is a universal term and does not necessarily refer to the same deity. What some people call "God" may in fact be "idols" and vice versa. So, the point being made here is, you need to find out if your partner believes in the same "God" as you. This is assuming you want to marry someone who believes in God, otherwise, this question is irrelevant.

10. To what extent is your current religious practice a part of your life and will that depth of involvement change after marriage?

The last thing you want to start doing with your partner after marriage is competing with their religion for a place in their lives. This question is to help you determine what is acceptable to you with regards to your partner's religion and how that is likely to affect their ties with you. You should remember that a person's religion is usually regarded as sacred and any action on your part that seems to threaten this sanctity is likely to put you in the wrong light.

11. Do you expect me to be involved in your religious practices? If so, to what extent?

This is a lot easier to deal with if you have similar religious affiliations. If it is new to you, the answers will help you assess the depth of your possible involvement and how well it sits with you.

12. When you were growing up, did your family belong to and regularly attend church, synagogue, temple, or mosque?

Wherever your partner was first introduced into religion, there is likely to be a seed of that religion planted in them and this can always grow again. They may have changed their spiritual orientation, but it is worth noting that they can always revert to their earliest experience, given the right opportunity.

13. Do you currently practice a different religion from the one in which you were raised?

This is a question to complement the previous one.

14. Do you believe in life after death? And why?

Again, this is another fundamental area where religions differ and the reason for asking about this is simple – the acceptance or not of life after death shapes their outlook and how they engage with certain aspects of life.

15. Does your religion impose any personal or behavioural restrictions that would affect our relationship?

Many religions have some restrictions that can affect matters relating to food, health, sexual relations and social engagements, among other things. It is good to know about these and identify prior to marriage which of them might affect your intimacy or general family life. Even among persons with the same religious orientations, spiritual interpretations can differ; therefore, it is not enough to be simply content that they are of the same religious orientation. You need to discuss these matters openly or you might be in for a rude awakening.

16. Do you consider yourself a religious person or spiritual person – what is the difference to you?

All I can say is that one is deeper than the other; one is about acts, the other is a lifestyle; one fills the need for belonging and the other is an effort to draw closer to a higher divinity in order to become better.

17. Do you engage in spiritual practices outside of organized religion in a church, synagogue, temple, or mosque?

This is an extension of the question above. For some people, spirituality ends with attending a church, mosque, synagogue or a Hindi service. They do not embrace their spirituality as a more intimate lifestyle, outside their religious centre.

18. How important is it to you for your partner and children to share your religious beliefs?

Here you are gauging how deeply their religion will be woven into the family fabric subsequent to marriage. Or are they happy for their spouse and children to freely choose their independent paths?

19. In what order of importance will you classify these: your religion, family, career and social life?

This is a very tricky question, nevertheless, one worth asking. You are likely to find out where you fall in their list of priorities, irrespective of whether or not you share the same religious orientation. .

20. How important is it to you for your children to be raised in your religion and will you grant them the right to choose at any time?

This is where you are going to find out whether or not your partner's currently practiced religion or spirituality has added any tangible value to them. If this is the case, then they would not only want to introduce their children to it but also, as far as is reasonably possible, make it a part of their lives.

21. As your future spouse, will I be required to operate within certain specific codes of conduct based on your religious orientation?

Some religions have certain specifications on how a husband/ wife ought to behave and although you are not yet married, you need to know in case these conflict with your own personal beliefs or expectations.

22. In a religious context, what is your understanding of love, respect, headship and submission?

Men crave respect and women, love. It is more than likely that if your partner is highly religious, their faith may have offered to them an "ideal" relating to love and respect. It matters little if they personally have a different take on these things because you can be sure that their religious beliefs will have a big influence on how they interpret and live out all of the above.

23. What would you say are the major differences between how you practice your faith and the manner in which others of similar faith practice theirs?

Yes, they may be Christian, Jewish or Muslim but within all of the world's religion you will find different sub-sects, schools of thought and doctrines. As such, it simply is not enough to be content that you both follow the same main religion. How the person practices their religion can be significantly different from what you expected or were prepared to embrace.

24. What are the three biggest changes that your religion has brought to your life since you started practising it?

If you are going to be a part of your partner's life and a religion is a part of theirs, it makes sense to get a glimpse of the tangible and progressive impact that their religion has brought to them to date as this could affect you too.

25. How does your religious orientation require you to view those who are not believers of your faith?

Well, if they accept what their religion teaches about unbelievers, then depending on what their religion does say about such persons, you could get a picture of how they are likely to view your family, friends and colleagues who are not aligned to their faith.

26. How does your religious orientation require you to engage in forgiveness and generosity?

Don't assume all religions teach on love, forgiveness and generosity. They may very well do, but from different perspectives and understandings as to their application.

27. Do you believe that people of different religious orientations can still go ahead and have a successful marriage?

In Christianity, it is very clearly stated "...do not be unequally yoked with unbelievers..." and other religions may say the same or otherwise. Asking this question has two benefits. On the one hand, it clarifies whether your partner is permitted to be with you or not. Secondly, if your partner decides to defy what their religion stipulates in order to be with you, you should then have an idea what they could revert to, IF they ever do – some religions may even list the consequences clearly.

28. Are there religious practices you engage in that conflict with your own views of life?

Because your partner is religious and adheres to the code of conduct of their faith, does not mean they do not exercise their own mental faculties, will or desires. Seeing where the latter conflict with the former for your partner, provides an insight into areas they find difficult to align with their faith.

29. How long have you been practicing your current faith and how much longer?

Surprise! Surprise! It is remotely possible that some people embrace a certain religion purely for exploration and to experience it for themselves temporarily without any intention of long-term commitment. It is crucial, therefore, to know if they are practising for reasons other than you normally would have imagined.

30. How did you come to embrace your current faith and what was the motivation for doing so?

The foundation on which anything is built determines largely how strong and how long what is built on it is likely to stand. Based on this premise, you should be examining the answers your partner gives with a view to determining if their motivation is inclined towards temporary or long term goals.

31. Does your religious belief make you feel isolated from any part of life and society?

Indeed, if your partner's religion encourages them to be mostly isolated, whether in real life or ideologically, then it should make sense to extrapolate such seclusion to your own possible circumstances when you get married.

32. What are your ultimate expectations from your current religion?

Every religion purports to offer a final reward, but truthfully, the religious or spiritual expectation that drives your partner, will to a large extent determine the temperament and consistency of their spirituality.

33. Do you pray, and if you do, how do you pray, to whom and what purpose does prayer serve in your general living?

Prayer is a major pillar of many religions. Knowing whether they do it at all and how it is, helps you to gauge your spiritual compatibility with them.

34. Do you believe it takes a combination of your personal efforts and God's input to be successful in life?

Now this might be a tricky one because some people profess faith, yet believe ultimately, their success depends totally on themselves it can be true vice versa. The answer will give you a sense of how much your partner is dependent on own efforts or spirituality to make life happen. There are two things you can spot here – a person who is either true to their faith and lazy, or true to their faith and responsible.

35. *Have you ever been affiliated to any religious movement that the rest of the world has labelled as "fanatic?"*

This question is to find out if your partner is a member of any organization branded as fanatic. If this is the case, you owe it to yourself to try and understand the philosophy and reasoning behind the organisation's actions in order to understand your partner's motivation.

36. *Have you ever been discriminated against on the basis of your religion?*

Any experience of this nature can leave psychological scars on your partner and in turn, affect you. An experience with discrimination can influence a person's future interaction with their own religion as well as that of others, including those that discriminated against them.

37. *Have you ever discriminated against anyone on the basis of their religious affiliations?*

Here, you are looking to see if latent tendencies exist for your partner to treat others in a certain way because of their religious affiliations. Even if this is exists but is not towards your immediate family and friends – keep it in mind, that if your family and friends fall in the discriminatory category of your partner, equally remote opportunities may exist for them to be discriminated against.

38. *In what ways, if any, do you feel threatened by other religions?*

This question looks at your partner's perceptions on how they may be treated by others as a result of their religious affiliations. It may not in reality turn out to be true, but it may well explain their openness or guarded interactions with people of certain other religious beliefs.

39. *How do you see your religion evolving and impacting the rest of the world over the next few years?*

As human beings, we evolve and although religious principles and tenets may remain unchanged, their interpretations and applications in a changing world are bound to differ depending on the times in which we are living. This question is first to test whether your partner recognizes this dynamic and secondly, if they do, to get a glimpse of how they are preparing to embrace that likelihood of future change.

40. *What do we do now in our relationship, that you feel can negatively affect your spirituality if we carry on into marriage?*

Religion and its requirements will always, in one way or the other, conflict with the dynamics of human society and daily living. Therefore, this question seeks to look at possible conflicts within such areas as family living, career, intimacy and as many other aspects of your daily lives as possible.

41. Tell me three things you would have done if you were not practicing your current faith?

You are obviously not finding out in order to use it against them. But truth be told, the practice of religion does place restrictions on us – for the good or at least this is the idea. Having these restriction does not, however, mean that your partner's natural urges which may conflict with their spiritual tenets will just disappear into thin air. The answers will help you understand the battles they deal with daily between their personal desires and their religious beliefs.

42. Is the life you live now fully consistent with the life prescribed by your religion?

If your partner is honest or feels you are trustworthy, they are likely to confide in you on where they are experiencing gaps in their alignment with the tenets of their faith. They may also claim not to have many gaps – it does not "always" mean they are lying – it may be they have reached a level of spiritual maturity that allows them to tame their personal desires. Whatever it is, you being close to them will be the best judge of it.

43. Which members of your family practice the same faith as you, and how long have they practiced it?

The tendency is that if your partner's faith is practiced collectively by their family, they are likely to stay in it longer due to the extra strength of family connections. It is not always the case, but it presents a high probability.

44. *Do you have a spiritual mentor or someone already practising your faith that you look up to?*

A mentor is obviously one who has already achieved what the mentee is aspiring to. If you can ascertain the spiritual attainment of your partner's mentor, you can form a picture of where their religious aspirations are headed.

45. *What is your favourite religious saying, song or poetry?*

Words - whether in the form of a poem, a song or prose - affect us all. The words that we are most connected to are those that express what we are or aspire to become. So even if your partner is not expressive, their favourite quotes can tell you something about who they are or desire to be.

46. *What has been your best and worst religious experience to date?*

This should be interesting. In fact it should well inform you about the two extremes of their religious engagements. It is somewhat a definition of their religious world.

47. What are the financial or money-related principles from your religion that you strictly adhere to?

You need to know since you do not want to have questions in marriage about approaches to money management based on different religious ideologies. This should be sorted out and agreed upon from the very beginning of your relationship.

48. If you were to go through very dark times in life, do you consider your faith sufficient to see you through it?

Sounds more like a self-assessment for your partner, doesn't it? Well, beyond that, it gives you an insight into how likely your partner will be able to make it through life's tough times. Having this knowledge should help you with ideas of what you might expect to deal with when those times come. And they will come, I guarantee you.

49. What would you do if you came to the realization I have spiritually backslidden?

It's easy to assume if you were married to a spiritual man or woman, that they will continue to be just that – spiritual. It's the easiest way to feel peaceful. The reality however is that in going through life's journey, this can change. There is no doubt about the possibility of this happening – what needs settling is whether you are mentally, emotionally and spiritually prepared for it and whether or not you have a plan if it does happen.

3

Professional, Social & Worldview

We are all socially interactive beings. I am of the conviction that a person's professional and social interactions do rub on their domestic demeanour. More often than not, your partner's profession is likely to occupy a large part of their daily life – it makes sense to soundly assume therefore, that if they feel reasonably fulfilled in their field of work and have a good balance between their professional, spiritual, social and family lives, then their general living, is likely to be one of soundness – these are what the bank of questions in this section seek to establish. It goes a step further to attempt gauging how their current rhythm of living is likely to evolve within and alongside our fast changing world.

1. *Are you currently or have you been recently employed?*

    You should ask this and more if you want to avoid marrying someone who does not believe in work or unprepared to support the home on marrying – it's different if you consciously decide it's alright to bear the sole breadwinner responsibility or you indeed have the money to accommodate. If it matters to you however, then find out if their unemployment is from reasonable choice, circumstances beyond their control or do you judge it to be laziness.

2. *What is your general view on hard work?*

    If they do not value hard work, they will likely not respect it. If they do not respect it, they will not engage in it, and lastly, they will not pass its attitude to your children. Persons with an aversion to hard work are also likely to look for "other ways" of making money to support themselves and the question would be – what ways?

3. *Are you currently doing any work in an area that you are most passionate about?*

    Over time, doing work you enjoy, not only guarantees fulfilment but also helps develop one's expertise more easily in the chosen field. This then provides a degree of job stability and security. That employment stability can subsequently lend a positive hand to the marriage.

4. *How do you see your career developing in the next five to ten years?*

Deliberate planning for the future is more likely to lead to personal fulfilment and success rather than expecting things to happen by themselves. The answer can give an insight into personal ambition and drive and whether the individual is likely to come to a halt if nothing works automatically for them or has enough personal drive to get up and make things happen. This kind of attitude is likely to reflect in marriage as the willingness to take responsibility for actions and inactions.

5. *Proportionately, what would be your ideal share of time between your work and your family?*

Deeply entrenched habits are hard to break, so take note of how they are handling their time right now. It is easy to say 'things will change when we get married – they usually don't. It may also be that they spend a lot of time at work but are able to spend good quality time with you, albeit short. You must consider that some people could also spend a lot of time with the family, but with little quality.

6. *Are you professionally very competitive?*

Competition is not necessarily a bad thing. At least it shows determination and a winning drive. If you personally are not the type to be self-motivated, then a competitive person may even inspire you one way or another. The real problem arises if the person is one who will stop at nothing to win in every circumstance. The last thing you want is for the mutuality in your marriage to become aggressive competition.

7. Is there any part of your career that you don't share because it could be disturbing?

What is acceptable to one person might be intolerable to another – hence, the need to ask a question like this; because what you might regard as a big problem might be considered perfectly normal by someone else. Be sure to ask, rather than assume because although you may not work directly with them, your marriage could make you an equal part of those acts.

8. Does your job involve a lot of travelling?

Distance separates individuals and can cause problems in marriage for some people. The frequency and length of business trips can put a strain on a relationship. You need to know what you can reasonably cope with, the nature of your partner's job and what it requires in terms of travelling. This way, you can know what to expect and discuss the matter in order to arrive at some reasonable agreement.

9. *Do you consider yourself a workaholic?*

You can partially deduce the answer to this one based on your own observations and the way your partner talks about their work. Getting a response from your partner is important. You may find out this only happens during certain peak times of the year, based on the demands of the job – not all year round.

10. *Do you have a financial retirement plan and how would you spend your retirement?*

It may seem far far away, but the truth is that most government pension schemes may not even sustain one's basic living standard upon retirement. For this reason, you had better start thinking about retirement early. This question could serve as a prompt to get your partner thinking about retirement if they haven't already. Forward planning is important to avoid or lessen the effect of certain preventable financial pressures on your marriage late in life.

11. *Have you ever been fired from your job?*

Handle this with care and if your partner was ever fired, listen carefully and deeply to what the reason was. If it turns out to be a repeated job loss issue, it could be an attitude problem or other genuine problems having nothing to do with your partner at all. If you suspect it is an attitude issue, consider the possibility the same might find its way into their personal and social life.

12. *What is your idea of fun and do you consciously take time to have fun?*

Like me, some people, by their very nature or as a result of how they were raised, are very serious about life. It is not that they do not want to have fun. Very likely, they do not know how and they need you to help them learn how to enjoy life. Just do not attempt to completely take their seriousness away from them. Offer help in small doses. It will be very unfortunate if you both take life very seriously as there will not be a lot of shared fun moments to hold on to when you need them later in life

13. *Does your work involve attending social functions? If so, will your spouse be expected to attend these functions with you?*

This is a very crucial piece of information worth knowing in advance, especially if you are the shy or very private type of individual – it is best to know and start preparing yourself for it. A compromise might be needed, as you cannot realistically attend all such gatherings.

14. *Do you harbour any racial, ethnic, political or social prejudices against any individual, people or organisations?*

When asking this question, assure the other party that you are only asking to know them better. If they have any of these prejudices, it will be wise to find out what they are and how they were developed. At least knowing both of these things should help you be on the look-out for situations that might lead to unpleasant confrontations around these prejudices. If the answers may affect their relationship with people close to you, then talk about it and have a plan on how best to diffuse the situation, if it arises.

15. *Are you the committed type who is always there for your friends?*

A person who answers in the affirmative is likely to be loyal. However, you also need to find out if they are willing to show loyalty even if the other party does not reciprocate. If they expect the same in return, they run the risk of being hurt because people rarely give back as good as they get. Let them know it is a good thing to be loyal to friends, as long as they settle in their own mind not to always expect the same in return. This is the only way to protect their heart.

16. *Upon marrying me, do you expect our individual friends to become our mutual friends?*

Sorting this out will prevent a lot of awkward encounters and explanations regarding friendships developed prior to marriage. When brought out into the open and some kind of mutual understanding is reached, at least each of you will know how to behave towards these friends to minimize conflicts.

17. *How easy would you find it to set limits in your relationships in order to devote attention to something you personally want to do alone?*

At times, matters relating to your relationship and family need to be restricted for various reasons. If the answer to this question shows signs of the individual's inability to draw the line on private matters, then there is need for a good discussion of the matter.

18. *Has friendship with others ever caused problems in any of your past relationships?*

If this has happened in the past, it is possible they have learned their lesson, but, on the other hand, maybe they have not, so history may repeat itself. Since you cannot assume – make a mental note.

19. *What are your favourite hobbies?*

This gives an insight into the balance between work and play. All work and no play can make your partner a very tense and an emotionally hard rock! That state of tensed emotion is bound to affect your relationship negatively too.

20. *How much money do you regularly spend on leisure activities?*

It shows to what extent they place value on their hobbies and leisure in general. Spending money for recreational activities should not be disallowed altogether. The concern should be with what proportion is spent on it.

21. Do you expect to have any time for yourself to go out with friends on a regular basis?

If this was their usual life before marriage, be careful not to cut it off suddenly. It would not be wise to do so as it can be wrongly seen as trying to control or rob them of their freedom. Your partner on the other hand, also needs to understand that when someone marries they cannot expect to be living like the single person they previously were. Adjustments must be made, new loyalties forged.

22. With what kind of people do you usually socialize?

Ever heard the expression "show me your friends and I'll tell you your character?" Well, it is actually very true – people of like minds tend to stick together. If they do not have friends at all, then that is also a problem, because they will be expecting you to fill in this gap, which places an extra burden on you. Find out if they need help learning how to socialize and show them how, because in every area of life we need to interact with others to be fulfilled.

23. When socializing, do you enjoy being the centre of attention or in the background?

The answer to this question is more to see if the person is inclined towards being an introvert or an extrovert - which could indicate the area in which you can complement their personality. This could be true in your situation, especially as it is usually said that opposites attract.

24. How involved are you in community activities where you live?

Involvement in community activities can spring from an altruistic nature or from a selfish one. You need to distinguish between the two. The person who gives altruistically is one that does so without any thought of reward. Such a person is generous and sacrificial in spirit and is always willing to help others improve themselves. By extension, such a person should be a caring and sharing partner.

25. Do you feel it is the responsibility of the haves of the world to help the have-nots?

For someone who holds this principle acceptable, giving and being benevolent is not likely to be seen by them as a disposition of choice but rather, one of responsibility. There is a good chance that level of inherent social responsibility on a personal level will reflect in your relationship.

26. Do you personally think change can only occur through violent means?

It is easy for anyone to opt for "non-violence" simply because it sounds morally correct. Your interpretation of the answer to this is most definitely going to be skewed by your own attitude towards violence. The truth, however, is that in some extreme circumstances diplomacy may not work – look out for balance. Their answer should give you an idea where they are likely to lean towards in deciding what solutions will fit certain social problems.

27. Do you consider yourself a law-abiding person and in what circumstances would you consider it alright to flout the law?

Look out for honesty, self-preservation and equally a willingness to consciously be either at loggerheads or at peace with the law. What you find out here, is very likely what you will get in marriage. So if for example you identify there is a tendency for your partner not to care about the "law," chances are that they will flaunt them even in marriage, thereby putting you at risk with themselves – by association.

28. Have you ever committed a crime or been arrested?

Bear in mind that after marriage, you both become part of each other's history and partake equally in the consequences of that history. You should be looking out for self-control, self-awareness, understanding of rights and responsibilities or ignorance of the law. Honesty to even disclose such information to you can be a plus in building trust.

29. *Have you ever been the victim of a violent crime?*

If the answer is yes, find out if they are willing to talk about it with you. If otherwise, do not insist. When they do tell you, however, listen carefully as there might still be scars from the encounter no matter how well they may seem to have overcome it. Then, do your best not to create circumstances that remind them of it when you get married.

30. *Would you say politically that you lean toward being a liberal, moderate, or conservative?*

This gives a hint into the general principles they believe in and which will most likely show up at home or in the general dealings of life. I suggest you have a quick read on what each of the two extremes of political ideologies mean.

31. *Do you belong to a political party and are you actively involved in it?*

Most people support political parties casually. If your partner has membership status, it can indicate that the person truly believes in the ideologies of that party. It also gives a hint of a tendency to be loyal.

32. *Do you believe that two people of differing political ideologies can still have a successful marriage?*

You can glean a lot here about their openness and ability to engage on issues irrespective of how much it differs from their own position. It may also be an indication of one's ability to separate business, political and social agendas from personal ones.

33. *Do you believe that all political systems show some amount of unfairness towards people in different kinds of social groupings?*

Some of these groups are people of colour, the poor, illiterates, women and the generally disenfranchised. Their answer can give you a hint as to whether or not they have a disposition to defend blindly or to accept the imperfections of man-made systems and by extension, their personal ability to accept or deny their own imperfections or wrongs during marriage.

34. *Which issues in society do you care about most?*

Some of these national issues include national security, privacy, the environment, the budget, human rights, women's and gay rights, among other things. Listen carefully to national issues that are closest to their heart, the chances are that the domestic equivalents of these will be the ones that matter most to them at home, during marriage.

35. *Has politics affected any of your past relationships?*

People have different degrees to which they are passionate about making change happen from a national or political perspective – for some, their relationships can be sacrificed if the latter appears to be an unwelcome competition for their political aspirations. It might not be a bad thing for your partner to aspire to public office, but it is certainly good for you to know this ahead of time. If their aspiration is alright with you, you can help them pursue their dreams in this direction. If you are not happy with it, you can make the case to them to reconsider, or failing that, start learning to adjust in case these aspirations become a reality.

36. *Do you have ANY political aspirations, no matter how remote they are?*

It may be hard for a lot of people to answer this for fear they may lose their relationship as a result. If you really want to know, you also need to provide some sort of assurance to your partner – that it will not affect your affection or commitment to them. You certainly want to know because you don't want to be taken by surprise in the future. It is also possible that these aspirations develop over time, but if they already exist albeit remotely – it is worth knowing.

37. *In what directions do you think the world is moving?*

Having a general understanding of where the world is heading vis-à-vis trends and innovations, shows whether or not your partner is conscious about changes around them and changes that must be made in their own life to adapt to those wider changes –personally, financially and career-wise. It suggests an awareness of the social environment and how this is likely to impact on one's success in all areas of life.

38. *Tell me what you think are some major socio-political changes that you think will happen in the world over the next five to ten years?*

Surely the world is changing very fast daily and its changes will impact the way we live and do things in it. It is important to be aware of these likely changes in areas such as politics, religion, technology, and health and family so we can prepare ourselves to cope with them and interact with them better. Relationships will always live within these social contexts and the changes in the latter will affect how relationships also evolve.

39. *How do you envisage we should specifically prepare our family for these future changes in the world?*

I think the best way is to discuss this in an exploratory manner so the two of you are taking a journey into the future – together. The aim of this question is to help both of you ready your relationship and family for the future. Yes it may sound futuristic but I believe there is good value in asking yourselves what changes are likely to come with the future and to attempt to match each of these with a strategy to deal with it. It's always comforting to be mentally ready for the future at least.

40. What are your general views on the peculiarities, strengths and weaknesses of the different continents of the world?

This s is a much more compartmentalized approach to capturing how your partner views the world in geographical blocs. Their views on these geographical blocs will no doubt influence their engagement with the cultures, people, economies, and opportunities of these blocs. If your marriage is situated say in a high culturally diverse environment and you both needed to interact with other cultures – you will from their answers here, understand why they will react in different ways to such different persons and cultures.

41. What lessons from your professional life have been most beneficial to your personal life and vice versa?

You are asking this to see whether or not your partner's life is lived compartmentalised – do they have a structured way of life that is strictly lived at work and another, strictly for intimacy and another for family and so forth? Or are they able to leverage different parts of their lives to cross-benefit all parts? This should help you manage the expectation that if you see them living a certain way at work, you shouldn't necessarily expect the same to be displayed at home too.

4

Past Relationships & Emotions

Being in a previous relationship could have two potential impacts on your potential marriage. On the one hand, there may have been positive lessons learned, which can be brought to leverage in your current relationship and subsequently, marriage. It could also (sadly) have produced bad experiences which if not handled well, could prevent one from fully opening up to the current relationship and later, in marriage. This section raises questions to help you access insights into where your partner is coming from (relationship-wise), the experiences they took away, how it may impact your current relationship with them and afterward, marriage and what to do. It may be tempting to skip this section if you haven't been in a prior relationship before, but don't – your partner may have been in one and it's still worth considering some of the questions here.

1. *How long ago was it between when our relationship started and your last one ended?*

   Normally, when one relationship ends, an emotional vacuum develops which many people just want to get filled – QUICKLY. The desire can be so strong that they simply jump into another one without taking time to step back and examine what went wrong with the last one and what ought to be done differently in the new. From my own experience, I usually recommend a 4-6 months break before getting into a new relationship.

2. *Would you say our relationship (i) helped you overcome your last relationship or (ii) is a fresh start for you, totally independent of your last relationship?*

   Following up on the previous question, this one is a little bit more specific in that it tries to clarify the motivation for the present relationship. If it is answered honestly, it should give you a glimpse into whether or not your relationship is independently relevant or is one that is necessarily filling a gap created by the ending of their past relationship.

3. *Have you been previously married?*

   This is the type of question, the answer to which is sometimes hidden until you actually ask. You are asking it because if they were, you should next be asking why they are no more. These two pieces of information should help you assess firstly whether you should be getting involved with them in the first place.

4. *If you were previously married, are you officially divorced?*
    It's one thing for your partner to say "it's complicated" or "things never worked between us," but you need concrete evidence of a divorce, if there was equally an official marriage. Otherwise, you are stepping on forbidden grounds. No matter what else they say, you need proof or else you proceed with the relationship at your own peril. I have personally seen relationships in which a partner swore, they were no more married only to get involved with a new person, have kids and their old spouse shows up to take their place in the family.

5. *Do you still have any form of relationship with your divorced partner, and if so, what is it?*
    There might be children involved or other reasons for contact to be maintained – you need to know in order for you to know if your partner's involvement with their ex is within or going beyond communicated boundaries.

6. *What was the reason for your divorce – from your and your Ex's perspectives?*
    While there are always three sides to every story, you need to listen and judge for yourself as best as you can, what the

real reasons for the dissolution of the previous marriage were. Even in the best of marriages, it is not guaranteed there would be no divorce. Do their explanations sound reasonable? Plausible? Unbalanced, is all the blame being placed on the other party? Does the explanation leave you feeling uncomfortable or assured?

7. *Do you have any children from any previous relationships?*
Yes, take nothing for granted. People do not always mention these things upfront until your heart is won and it becomes difficult for you to back out. Asking early is a sure way to prevent your heart from becoming engaged before it is too late. After all, very few people come on their first few dates with their children in tow!

8. *If you have children from a prior relationship, who has legal custody of them?*
The courts may not always be fair in terms of who takes custody of children in a marital breakdown. This is not just about the care of the children. From your partner's responses, you can gauge their attitude toward children – whether they are yours or not.

9. What is your current relationship with your child and how do you expect that relationship to evolve after we get married anew?

Look out for some humanness, honesty, care. They may not have custody of their child but see if they are willing to maintain some connection – or have they totally disconnected from their child and why? Always have this at the back of your mind, that it was never the child's fault to be born. But of course, all the above questions will depend on your own comfort level with possibly caring for a child who is not yours. How do you feel about this?

10. Other than marriage, how many serious relationships have you had before me and are you still connected to anyone from those relationships?

Just like a job market, the more relationships one has had and the more short-lived they have been, the greater the cause for concern about the commitment level of the person and their stability in relationships. Nevertheless, give them the benefit of doubt and explore on a case by case basis, why their last relationship may have failed to go the distance.

11. What percentage of your past relationships has been sexually intimate?

Here is a truth not a lot of people want to hear – for anyone you engage with sexually, an emotional bond is created. A soul tie is established. It is easy to simply say" we are not seeing each other anymore" – but it does not necessarily dismantle those emotional and soul bonds. Over time and depending on how many persons they have been with, one's soul and emotions can become a web of many criss-crossing wires – even though they want to move on genuinely with someone new.

12. Are you prepared to have a test for Sexually Transmitted Diseases before we marry?

Love or no love, you both need to be tested in these days of casual sex and so many opportunities to pick up STDs. If your partner is infected, so will you – sadly you cannot tell if they are infected from their physical appearances alone. Being tested is for the safety of both of you. While in some pre-marital counselling sessions it is optional, in others, it is mandatory along with testing for sickle cell disease. Taking any of these tests can be life-saving! Do not just talk about it – do it.

13. Did any of your past relationships end in particularly bitter manner?

This may leave bad memories, if it happened. What you are doing with this question is finding out which areas of your own relationship with your partner might be affected by these past experiences. For example, if their bitter experience was finding out their Ex was unfaithful, then trust becomes a big thing for them and it may require your constant assurance to keep them confident that you would never do something like that.

14. Is there any physical object that you still keep with you from any of your previous relationships ?

This may be trivial, but it could be an indication that your partner might still be harbouring emotional connections with someone in their past and finding it hard to let go. An action of this sort speaks louder than their words to the contrary.

15. Have you got unresolved issues between you and anyone from your past relationships?

I suggest this question because the last thing you really want is to be in a relationship with your partner and yet, someone in their past, still has a justified reason to hold them hostage either financially, emotionally, spiritually – that's effectively power to ruin your happiness at will.

16. Do you know of anyone you have ended a relationship with who claims to still love you and will do anything to get you back?

There are hardly a lot you or your current partner can do about this, but you should be aware of the fact that love is a strong emotion and when it is lost it can drive some people to take extreme actions to try and recover this affection. This makes it worth knowing so you are mentally prepared for any future events.

17. What attracted you most to the person in your last relationship?

It may be a lot more relaxing for them to talk about a past partner because s/he is not there to hear and object. Chances are, they are looking for the same thing in you too. It may not always be the case, nevertheless, chances are it is to some extent.

18. Did you suffer abuse of any kind in any of your former relationships?

If this has happened, some of that experience will stay with them and it will by most likely influence similar aspects of your current relationship with them.

19. Have you in any past relationship, come close to getting married, and if so, what happened?

You are asking because it may or may not be a gauge for yourself in assessing your own chances of proceeding to marriage. Whatever the case, at least the answers will high-light to you what issues are crucial to them, enough to spell a marriage "no-show."

20. What did you cherish most from your previous relationships if any at all?

No matter how long their former relationship lasted (if any), it would have done so because some good things happened. They are worth knowing because they have certainly contributed to the successful part of their past relationship and could very well contribute to yours with them.

21. Would you say that there is a similarity in the type of individuals you dated in the past?

This question re-enforces the previous one - only that it looks at the issue from a different angle.

22. Do you intend to keep an open friendship with any of your past partners?

You are not forbidding them maintaining such a relationship rather trying to understand why they wish to keep it going. It is in your interest to want to understand the nature of such a continuing connection since it could impact on yours.

23. Have you been in touch very lately with anyone from your past relationships?

It may have happened by chance or intentionally. There is nothing wrong with either – you simply want to understand the motive behind this.

24. *Do you intend inviting anyone from you previous relationship to our wedding?*

You are asking this based on any discomfort you may have of Exs attending your wedding. If your partner doesn't see anything wrong with it, then some talks needs to happen.

25. *To what extent are you likely to help a previous partner from a past relationship?*

This is not to establish to what extent your partner hopes to engage regularly with persons from their past relationship, rather it seeks to address the "one off" occurrence that might sometimes arise.

26. *Do you have any contractual or mutually agreed obligations to anyone from your past relationships?*

The usefulness of this question is that if your partner's involvement with persons from past relationships goes beyond "voluntary" to obligatory, they have to fulfil them. This might include moral as well as legal commitments. If this is the case, it is in your best interest to consider helping your partner to dutifully and quickly discharge such obligations.

27. Do you still have any shared interests in financial or non-financial assets with anyone from your past relationships?

This is linked to the previous question and it seeks to establish a good reason for continued contact and relationship with past partners.

28. Is there anyone from your past relationships that you would have loved to remain as our mutual friends?

If you do not think you would be comfortable about it, then this question creates the genuine platform for you to say so. But beyond that, it clears the air as to how your partner expects you to relate to such friends.

29. Are there any secrets about any of your previous relationships that if I found out, could jeopardise my trust for you?

This is more of a mitigating question or one for future damage control in that your knowing the secret now could save you from feeling betrayed if others should bring it to light later.

30. What has been the one area of your past relationships where there has been the most tension, arguments and misunderstandings?

These could represent high risk areas in your own relationship with your partner, and which you may want to understand more thoroughly in order to guard against them or minimize them as much..

31. *Would you say you are mostly drawn to younger, older or same age partners?*

People say age is just a number but this is not entirely true. Some men think a considerably younger woman will help sustain their intimate passions. Some women believe men of their similar age may not be as mature as they would like them to be, while other persons might have many other varied ideologies. Knowing what category your partner has been most comfortable with and which you fall in, is certainly useful information either to buttress their choice in you or question it.

32. *Have your previous partner(s) been religious?*

The religious orientation and commitment of your partner is of paramount importance to your future life together because a person's belief shapes their life choices and actions. You will need to ask this question to determine if there is the likelihood of conflicts arising due to disparities in religious beliefs and orientations.

33. *To what extent would you say you are attracted to persons with intellectual dispositions very much like yours?*

The response is not necessarily a request for you to change. But it is helpful in preliminarily self-assessing whether or not you fall in their range of "usual" preference. Then again, their preferences may have over time been based simply on what they have been used to.

34. *Would you say you are normally a jealous person?*

If the person is given to jealousy this is not likely to change overnight. Furthermore, jealousy can be a sign of more serious underlying issues of insecurity and a desire to control which can make a relationship a very unhappy one. Consider further.

35. *What would a former partner honestly say are your strengths?*

People are naturally happy to talk about how "good" they have been painted to be. It should provide you with further insight into what they have been like in the light of past relationships. The information can also be a tool for you to use in checking whether your own assessment of your partner so far is consistent with what they have always been, or different.

5

Family Connections

If you are about to get married to your partner, then understand that they have, since being born, spent the most part of their life, with their respective family (whether natural, adopted, single or now separated). These are the persons who have in large part, shaped their natures, habits, views on life, family and marriage. There are some things you can only better understand about them if you understood their family background and how they have previously and currently interacted. This section contains a diary of appropriate questions to help you do that. Most especially, you will get a good sense of your partner's most ingrained picture of marriage, family and general life, born from what they've experienced since childhood.

1. *What are your parents' opinions about me?*

   Hopefully by now, your in-laws to be have met you. How you are perceived by your partner's parents is very important since your relationship with your in-laws is crucial to the success of your marriage. It is, therefore, good to have a heads-up signal from your partner on know how they see you.

2. *What are siblings and extended family's opinions about me?*

   This is an extension of the above question but provides a broader picture, as sometimes, not only parents, but also siblings and the extended family could be a very important part of (or influence over) your partner's life. In this case, knowledge about their opinions can help in your relationship building with them.

3. *Is there a particular way I should deal with each of the members of your family in order to maintain a good relationship with them?*

   If winning the hearts of your potential in-laws is a priority for you, then this is the question to dwell on. One good reason out of many many others, is that they know your partner better than you do (at least, until now) and a good alliance with them can be hugely beneficial not only for the purposes of knowing your partner more, but also for future support in your marriage.

4. *Are there any hereditary diseases in your family that might affect us and our children?*

Better to know this now and weigh your options rather than to find out afterwards. While such knowledge might not affect your decision to marry your partner, you should know the likely possibility of its effect on your new family's health or expected lifespan and the chances of the disease being passed on to the next generation.

5. *What is your relationship with your parents like?*

How a person relates to their parents can be a strong indicator of the nature of any relationship they might have, especially in marriage. A good healthy relationship with parents can signal a similar one in marriage and the opposite applies too. Unresolved relationship issues within their family can be carried over into marriage. Not only should you ask about this, but if the occasion presents itself, observe first-hand how they treat and interact with their parents.

6. *What is your relationship with your siblings like?*

Your partner's family and their relationship with them over time is their first training ground for developing healthy social interactions as members of a family. Eventually, it will influence all other relationships. How they have maintained this relationship over time will also say a lot about the person.

7. *Who are you closest to in your family and why?*

   This could bring out some interesting revelations, especially the part about why someone is their favourite. It could suggest some of the priority areas that are critical to them in relationships.

8. *How connected have you been with your extended family?*

   Some people will maintain family bonds t because of their natural disposition to do so, while others will do it solely out of duty. The former case will certainly be a strong indicator of the commitment of the person, when it comes to family.

9. *What have been your best memories of your family?*

   Those memories are most likely going to influence the memories they will be looking forward to create with their own family. It is a natural tendency to reinforce their own memories. It will mean there are certain activities they will be more inclined to participate in more than others, in building the new family

10. *Are there any peculiar patterns concerning marriages in your immediate or extended family?*

    Some families have a pattern of divorce or childlessness or other such things. They could be good patterns and not-too-good patterns. Since history tends to repeat itself, although there is no guarantee that it will in your time, it is good to know as this can provide a chance of avoiding, changing or preparing for it.

11. *Have there been divorces or single parenthoods that you know about in your wider family?*

There may be the occasional case and that is generally to be expected in families. However, it should be a matter to consider important if some trends appear to have been repeated several times.

12. *Has polygamy ever been a part of your larger family practices?*

If the practice of polygamy was part of the environment your partner grew up in, it is likely to be considered normal by them, unless they have been out of that environment for a considerable amount of time or they have been immersed in a stronger, but different culture. However for some, while the urge to embrace the practice might have been suppressed, the inherent tendency usually remains. It is always helpful to know whether or not the seeds of polygamy exist inherently or not.

13. *How have men generally turned out in your wider family?*

You may not necessarily be a spiritual person reading this book, but if you are, you are more likely to understand this: when you come from a family, you do not only walk away with genes – that's only biological. You will also very likely walk away with the "untouchable or spiritual" characteristics or heritage of that family. The question is being asked because how persons have turned out may have nothing to do with the physical but everything to do with the spiritual.

14. How have women generally turned out in your wider family?

This is simply the flip side of the preceding question.

15. What has been the best part of your growing up as a child?

In listening to the answer to this question, try to decipher why it was the best part of growing up. Listen out for peculiarities like the location, the economic status of the family at the time, and the nature of the activities and the people who were involved. Also look out for the tone of excitement with which particular aspects the information is conveyed. If they still remember those moments with great enthusiasm, it is possible those things will still inspire them now, as they did back then and that they are most likely to be the experiences they would want their new family to have.

16. Is your parents' marriage one you would like to have for yourself?

The parents' model of marriage is probably the only one your partner has known all their life and so it will most likely have shaped what they are looking forward to in their own marriage. More importantly, it would have influenced their idea of what a wife or husband should be like. If the parents' marriage was a good one, then there might be little to fear, but if it was a dysfunctional one, there are likely to be further clarifications you need to consider.

17. *Are there any vows or covenants that you have with your family?*

This refers largely to the spiritual aspects of life. Vows and covenants do not just go away because someone has left their parents' house or because they might have given back the symbols (e.g. signet rings) of the covenant. Despite doing this, the covenant still stands until it is properly renounced. Your partner should seek spiritual counsel to free themselves from any such covenants or vows.

18. *What is your blood group and type?*

I feel every person about to enter marriage should make this information available to their partner. If for some reason (e.g. Sickle Cell) your coming together may drastically affect your children, having a blood test done becomes even more crucial. While many of us believe that loves conquers all, it does not save you from the pain of sickness and disease, especially when it results from something that could have been avoided.

19. Are there specific responsibilities you will still be obligated to perform to your family even after getting married?

People have different notions about what it means to be married. For some, it means leaving their parents entirely to fend for themselves and, for others, it may mean retaining certain levels of responsibilities towards their parents. You should both clarify this so that it does not become a source of contention. Different family traditions might lead to expectations and obligations on the part of your partner that may not be acceptable to you. Take nothing for granted, raise the issue and get a clear understanding of what pertains.

20. Are there any crucial family ties you need to rebuild before we get married?

Are there some bridges that need to be re-built because they will be needed in the future? One such bridge is the relationship with parents and siblings. If any damage has been done to any such relationship between your partner and their immediate family, it may be worth encouraging them to mend the bridges. Some of the people involved in your partner's broken bridges may be the very people from whom you may need the blessings of marriage.

**21. *How did your parent (of the same sex as you) resolve
conflicts with your other parent, when you were growing?***

Parents are, consciously or unconsciously children's first role
models and this applies to marriage and how they resolve
conflicts too. A father usually serves as the role model for the
boys and the mother for the girls. This can be very revealing
and a hint to how they are likely to resolve conflicts in their
own marriage to you. Your partner may have evolved differently but you will sure see signs of their respective parents in
handling conflict.

**22. *Are there important family traditions that you want
continued in your family when you get married?***

Some families have traditions that knit them together, such
as Christmas and re-unions. Granted that you will be married to your partner and start your own family, you should
not be surprised that you will still be required to be part of
their larger family traditions. It can be a good thing as it
affords the opportunity to strengthen the bond between you
and their family, thus also creating good support for your
marriage and your children.

**23. *Is there any member of your family that opposes our
getting married?***

Family opposition to a member's choice of marriage partner
is not new. It happens all the time. If we wish to be honest,

we must admit that sometimes love does blind us to many things about our partner and it usually takes someone else to point out the likely danger spots. If your partner's family raise objections, try and find out why. Conversely, it might be your family. In both instances, instead of being angry, try and see if there is any validity in the reasons given. There might be some truth in what is being said although at times, the objections might arise from purely selfish reasons.

24. What have you learnt from earlier marriages in your larger family that you think will be useful to us in our marriage?

The good thing about some people travelling the same road before you is that you can avoid making the mistakes they made, if you learn from them. So looking at other marriages and drawing wisdom from them can be beneficial to you both when your time comes. This goes for the good as well as bad things.

25. What's been the trend with families on your father's side in terms of family matters?

This includes things like family size, number of children according to gender, the socio-economic status, any recurring pattern of death of child or spouse, and such things. This is a good opportunity to learn as much about their family and the environment in which they grew up. It should also help you explore some of the less obvious trends that exist in the family that could very well be mirrored in your own family.

26. What's been the trend with families on your mother's side in terms of family matters?

This is simply a follow-up from the previous question.

27. What are some of the things that your family believe and practice that you no longer do?

This is where you might start seeing the depth of change that has happened in your partner's life with regard to what they believe and do now in comparison to how they were previously raised. Be prepared for them not to change in some areas while in others they have totally moved away from parental beliefs and practices. Depending on what areas of their life changes have happened, it might be for the better or the worse.

28. Have you and your siblings been raised together throughout your childhood?

Siblings growing up together is the natural setting in which they learn healthy social interactions, to appreciate togetherness and to develop loyalty to family. Usually, this is reflected in their later relationships with others. On the other hand, growing up separated from siblings and family may impact

a person negatively and show up similarly in future relationships.

29. **What were the areas of priority in your family when it came to: education, family, religion, social status and wealth?**

All families tend to place emphasis on different aspects of life and this trend is likely to be passed on generationally. Whether your partner continues to follow this pattern will depend on how much they have embraced an alternative set of values as well how obviously successful their family may have become by following certain priorities.

30. **Do you know of any criminal history within your immediate or extended family and what are they?**

We all see movies of innocent persons courted and wed by crime bosses only for the former to find this out afterward when it is too late to do anything about it. So while some crimes might be minor and can be overlooked, you need to know if your partner's family is or has been involved in any crimes. There is such a thing as guilt or reputational risk by association. Your credibility or reputation (and therefor opportunities) may be ruined if you find out too late that the family you marry into has a criminal disposition or history..

31. *Is any member of your family in a position of high public office or socially considered as a public figure?*

Just as in the point above, if there is anyone in the immediate family of your partner who is in the public limelight, then you might find yourself in the news one day. How does this happen? Sometimes, when newsmakers are looking for a story and they cannot find one directly dealing with the public figure, they are likely to resort to someone with even the remotest connection to that person. You might thus find yourself a target for the media and so you need to plan ahead how you will handle this and make sure you behave discretely in case unpleasant things about you are made public.

32. *What are you most proud of about your family?*

People will always want to belong to something they can be proud of and families are no exceptions. When your partner answers on what things they are proud of about their family, it is very likely a hint of the kind of story they would like told about their own family someday.

33. *What is the religion of your family?*

If your partner's family has a deep religious orientation, there is a high probability your partner will share the same faith even if they seem to reject or deny this. Therefore, you should expect them to reflect some aspect of their parent's religion, even if it is not with the same intensity. Religious seed sown early in life do not die easily; they often linger, waiting for a chance to spring to life again.

34. *What has been the most trying moment in your family's history and how was it overcome?*

If the family has had one of such trying moments and survived it, it would have taught your partner that families, by standing together can always overcome challenges. It is often thought that families that firmly stick together even after serious troubles, often grow stronger in their bonding after the difficult circumstances.

35. *If everyone in your family was asked to be unanimous in a description of you, what three adjectives would they use to describe you?*

Listen to this answer very carefully. Up until this point, these are the people who have collectively known your partner better than any other group of people. When they describe your partner, they know in absolute terms who they are describing.

36. *Will the current bond with your family in any way affect the establishment of your own family?*

Family bonds run deep and sometimes the individual finds it difficult to break these bonds in order to establish their own family albeit that breakaway is the foundation for a new family. It takes tact and discretion by anyone to create the needed space while still maintaining good relations with your partner's wider family. One thing to keep in mind and prepare for is – in some circumstances, you may be seen as forcibly taking their son/daughter from them.

37. If your family were to feel at any time that I was not treating you the way they would, how do you think they would react?

I doubt you will set out to treat your partner in a bad manner. But whether or not you do, is often based on perception of your partner's family and not reality. Nevertheless, in case your partner's family sees you as not treating their child or relative right, you might want to know what would be their reaction so you can plan on how to handle it.

38. How is your family likely to react if after marriage, you needed my opinion to give help to them that you would have offered in the past without consultation?

This question can be used to gauge your partner's ability to establish new boundaries for their wider family. If it does actually happen, it will also serve as a good test to your partner's wider family on whether they recognize their new obligations to their child who is now married, not single.

39. *Based on your knowledge of me, is there anything you think will make it easy or difficult for your family to accept me?*

Your partner knows both you and their own family and so is in a position to answer the two aspects of this question. They are able to tell you where the personality clashes are likely to occur and other such landmines when dealing with their family. It is not the kind of information usually offered voluntarily, but it is definitely needed to help you negotiate the unknown waters represented by your future in-laws.

40. *What are some of the ways to win the hearts of your parents and siblings?*

Here we are talking the specifics things you can do to make them accept you into the family. Knowing these things could also serve as a future guide as to how to quickly repair broken relationships with any of them.

41. *What are the biggest likes and dislikes of each member of your family?*

Maintaining the path that leads to the hearts of your in-laws will help you define the boundaries of your relationship with them and this, prevent unnecessary conflicts.

42. *Are there decisions regarding our marriage on which you will have to consult your parents or the rest of your family?*
Yes, these things do happen and yet, most people will only find out about it after they have been married. In certain cultural contexts, larger family consultations are expected and accepted. You might feel like the in-laws are trying to interfere with the independence of your marriage, but you should try and understand the reasoning behind such practices – viewed objectively, it might make sense!

43. *Do any of your siblings look up to you in any area of your life?*
Younger siblings tend to look up to the older ones as benchmarks in modelling their own lives. Being aware of this kind of relationship and expectations from your partner can help you realize that your lives together serve as a role model for others. This should motivate you to work harder to make sure your marriage is successful since this will influence others one way or the other.

44. *If you already have children, have you informed them of wanting to marry me and how have they taken the news?*
This cannot be glossed over. Step-children can cause an endless set of problems that can ruin a marriage – they can also give it all the cooperation to make it very successful. Younger ones might see you as the person who took away their real

father or mother or as trying to replace them – if they have reason not to agree with your relationship. Either view breeds hostility. Older children might see you as a challenge to their inheritance and might reject you simply for that. If there is hostility, you will need to decide how you are going to cope with it or if you even want to venture down this path. Better still, stop, have it sorted, and then move forward. This matter needs to be carefully discussed as well as boundaries set for how you will interact with these children – young or old.

45. *What are your own expectations with regards to your relationship with my parents, siblings and any other close family members?*

Here is where the coin is flipped. I think what is said will be an indicator of how much approval your partner perceives they have from your family and how much they feel accepted by them. From both sides, parental and general family acceptance is a very important factor in a successful marriage because of the important role family plays in a person's life.

6

Sex, Love & Intimacy

Intimacy, no doubt is what keeps a couple bonded strongest. Contrary to what many assume – it doesn't just function naturally, it requires work and effort to keep going and even more work when children come into the picture. The purpose of this section is to help you two explore your different types of naturally occurring modes of intimacy, how to sync them, as well as identifying past present or future factors that could detract its smooth continuation and enjoyment. Finally, and best of all, some of the questions in this section should help you figure out how best to enjoy intimacy together. If your partner to whom these questions are being posed has never had any sexually intimacy before now, then skip the questions that are based on such an assumption. If you haven't yourself - don't worry, you haven't missed out.

1. *Have you had any unusual experiences with sexual intimacy that you like to avoid in marriage?*

    Sex during marriage is meant to be thoroughly enjoyed. Some however cannot enjoy it in full or in part because of some unusual experiences they have had in the past that may have left some scars on their memories. Knowing exactly what it is can help you navigate this delicate part of your relationship and, perhaps, even help turn a previous negative experience into a blissful one.

2. *Have you in the past or recently had a Sexually Transmitted Disease (STD)?*

    For a variety of reasons, you really want to know this. It is possible to contract STD's on one's first sexual encounter, so having it in the past may not necessarily mean that your partner was promiscuous. Your priority here is to establish whether they currently have any STD and if possible, get them to do a full test. Ideally, this should be mandatory because you are putting your life at risk if there is no full disclosure.

3. *Have you ever carried out a virility or fertility test very recently?*

    If children are very important to you, then this question should equally be. Infertility is one of those distressing encounters to have after marriage. Advisably it is a reassuring move for both of you to have tests done – but you both have to agree on it. I know Christians will ask about the place of faith in all of this and my response is - only you know the level of your faith in God and what He is telling you to do. According to your faith, so be it. My comments come from a rational approach based upon knowledge and real experiences of many others. It is up to you to decide what step you will take to address the situation. Or if you both feel that finding out early may be more distressing, then by all means, the choice is yours.

4. *How do you generally feel about who should initiate sexual intimacy?*

It is likely to become clear who is very traditional and who is very open-minded in their thinking about sex. Culture can have a great deal to play in this too. Do not wait till it is too late to find out that either your sexual preferences are being inhibited or that they are being violated – as a result of your partner's preferences in this regard.

5. *Tell me some things about sex you would like to explore when you get married?*

One of the reasons people cheat is because their sexual lives with their spouses become stale. You must both be willing to explore new dimensions of sex from time to time, otherwise it soon becomes a stale one-way routine. When that happens, any of you can become an infidelity risk. Any probability that a more exciting sexual encounter could be found with someone else becomes an infidelity trap.

6. *How do you see the role of sex – purely as a medium for procreation or mutual enjoyment?*

   For married couples, sex is for procreation, first and foremost and also for bonding and intimacy. It is never unilateral – it is always dual. The answer to this will immediately let you know whether your sex-life with your partner will be somewhat stale after children are had or that it has a chance to become better as time goes by and beyond the procreation of children.

7. *What is it that turns you on sexually?*

   Whether you are a man or a woman – an honest answer to this question empowers you to provide the kind of sexual experience your partner wants. You should mutually discuss this topic together and be brutally honest about it. There is no room for shyness or modesty here- this is the person you are promising to share your body, soul and spirit with in the most intimate union known to man. Tell it like it is and take good notes. You will be glad you did.

8. ***Do you have reservations about when and where to express
    any form of intimacy with your spouse?***

    Surprise surprise! Some people will express all the intimacy
    they can find in the world at home – but never outside its
    four walls. Why? It could be due to their cultural or religious
    orientation. In not-too-rare scenarios, it could even be a
    self-confidence issue. If being able to express your intimacy
    at all times is important to you, this is a starting point for
    such a discussion.

9. ***Are there times or periods that you will prefer not to be
    sexually involved with your spouse?***

    A religious person might want to stay away from sex during a
    period of fasting or other such times. It will be useful to come
    to a mutual understanding about the timing of these periods
    and how long they are likely to last.

10. ***Tell me some things you do not like about sex or would
    rather not engage in during sex***

    You need to be clear about these, so as not to reduce your
    partner's sexual pleasure. You should also mention anything
    along these lines that will also affect you negatively.

11. *What do you consider as reasonable in terms of the frequency of love-making?*

The physiology and chemistry of you and your partner is different, so what one might consider as too much sex, the other may consider as too little or enough. The agenda here is to arrive at what both of you will consider as a reasonable level of sexual frequency. You don't want one partner overfed sexually and the other, starved. Having settled that, allowances must be made for unexpected events and hormonal surges that might not make it possible to stick to what was agreed. Let's be realistic, you can't expect to FIX the number of sexual engagements together. Consider there will be an inability to meet such a commitment sometimes, due to fatigue or stress and not to mention, pregnancy and children. Consider also that there will be times when passions are high and intimacy becomes very necessary for expression.

12. *Do you have any particular health or emotional conditions that sexual activities might aggravate?*

Again, the thinking here is simple. Sex happens and then it is over, but emotional and health issues can linger on a bit longer. What you do not want is for your partner to start seeing sex as akin to pain rather than an intimate pleasurable connection between the two of you. Thus, you need to find out if there are any past negative emotions stirred up by sex or any health conditions that might decrease the pleasure of the experience.

13. What are your views on the use of contraception in marriage?

Contraception is a thorny issue for some, due to religious or cultural upbringing or related stigma. It also has to do with the number of children you really plan to have and how you intend to space them out. This is of particular importance to women on whom the burden of pregnancy falls. So it might be alright for a man to want ten children—but is the woman prepared to become pregnant ten times? How will this affect her career and her ability to care for so many children at one time? There is room here for a lot of discussion to arrive at consensus.

14. What are the most sexually sensitive parts of your body?

This is to kick-start your sexual enjoyment of each other's body when you marry and it is the only way you are going to develop a thorough knowledge of what your partner enjoys most. Please note, this is only the beginning, it should not end there. You are asking because you want to start right and continue to explore more and more into the marriage.

15. How important is my physical appearance to you?

Well, there was certainly an element of physical attraction when you first met and I think it really is a matter of choice if you want to keep that first time spark going throughout your marriage – highly recommended. How you dress generally and, more importantly, in the bedroom can affect your relationship. Some people get careless about their personal appearance and hygiene after they are married and for some, after they've had children but remember every day, your spouse sees attractively dressed people around them – you need to keep up with the efforts to remain attractive. Men have to be reasonable in considering also that after a childbirth, a woman's body does go through considerable physiological and chemical change.

16. How easy or difficult is it for you to apologize for a wrong done?

Saying I am sorry is extremely hard for some people because it requires admitting a wrong. Some are quick to apologize for things not even their fault in order to end a conflict. Repeated failure to ever say one is sorry is usually a sign of pride or insensitivity. Being able to say I am sorry is a mark of humility, maturity and an indication that the person wants to make a relationship work.

17. *How readily would you be willing, to take on the blame in a standoff, just so it doesn't get prolonged?*

Depending on what you find out, you may end up extending a separate question to yourself – "should I be the one to do this always? And if so, am I willing to do this?"

18. *How do you normally react when you are angry?*

This is very important. Not everybody flares up when angry. And if you don't know your partner is angry, then it gets more risky – risky because their anger is likely to pile up until it gets to a level where its expression can become explosive. If you do not know how your partner behaves when angry, you might also react in a manner (unknowingly perhaps) that adds to their aggravation. While we all can get angry, if it becomes a recurring pattern and/or your partner is abusive or threatening at these times, you need to take note and ask yourself some more questions. It helps to be in a relationship with someone for a good-enough time before rushing into marriage.

19. *Would you consider using sex as a tool to express your being upset or as a means of resolving an issue between us?*

Some people argue that it is not right to use sex as a tool to punish or reward your spouse in any given situation. It is as open to debate just as some people would employ sex to settle disagreements. Some may see it as manipulation. The two parties involved, based on their personal beliefs, will need to decide what works best for them when they are faced with both scenarios.

20. *What are some major things that you do not think you could ever forgive me for doing?*

Yes, there are certain boundaries that take us beyond our human ability to forgive. If you are both spiritual people, then you might be able to transcend your humanity and act out of the divine power within you to still forgive. But from a totally human perspective, there are limits beyond which we are not prepared to forgive. For example, some consider cheating as the final limit and they will walk away from a marriage because of this. Finding out what is regarded by your partner as an unforgiveable deed is important to the survival of your marriage.

21. *In order of importance, which of these words best defines "love" for you: commitment, trust, attraction, spiritual oneness, a decision, and feeling?*

Love means different things to different people and so you need to see how much you agree with your partner's definition of this magical and inexplicable thing that is often so hard to pin down. How one defines love drives how they engage with the different aspects of Love.

22. Do I have to earn your trust or am I automatically considered trustworthy until I break that trust?

Trust is an important cornerstone of any relationship, especially marriage. It is therefore helpful to know if your partner trusts you instinctively or if it must be earned. Neither approach is wrong in itself, but it is good to know where you stand and of course, you must guard this trust as a delicate treasure, because once broken, it is very difficult for it to be restored.

23. In what ways are we fundamentally different and how can these differences affect our relationship?

You are seeking here to find out the positive and negative effect of your differences on each other. A lot depends on the fundamental nature of the differences and the fact that some can be changed and others cannot. If there are too many negative influences caused by your differences, then you might need to re-consider your relationship, because people do not basically change overnight. In the end, you must determine if you have enough net positive differences to make your relationship meaningful and satisfying.

24. Is divorce ever an option for you in a marriage?

Some people do not consider divorce as an option in marriage; for others it is a last resort when things go terribly wrong and for some, it is just the natural path to go once things move in a direction they do not like. A lot of this is going to depend on each other's personal core values that come from religion, family upbringing or the views held by the society one is influenced by. Whatever the response, it will raise issues of loyalty and commitment to marriage and this should be aired thoroughly between you, even though you hope it never happens.

25. Do you believe that people should stick in marriage even if they are unhappy, as long as no violence is involved?
This is simply a different angle to the preceding question but with a bigger opportunity to get a sense of your partner's views.

26. What is the best way and time to raise an issue with you about something you have done or said that upsets me?
Communication is crucially key in your relationship and quite easily, a communication strategy that works more times than it fails is extremely useful. This is a good way to know, from the start, what communication techniques work best with your partner since you are hearing it directly from them.

**27. *If apart from love, friendship was all we had to go on,
would this be strong enough to keep us together?***

After the initial passions are quenched some time later in the
marriage, it requires friendship and a deep sense of commitment to keep the marriage going. Therefore, along with the
passionate loving, there should be a solid friendship between
you which ensures that you actually like and enjoy each other's company. So if you have not already established a real
friendship, you need to be developing that now.

**28. *Are you comfortable allowing yourself to be vulnerable
around me?***

This is to help you determine whether your partner is emotionally "fully" committed to you – it has nothing to do with
whether they love you or not. Until someone can come to
that place where they can be at their weakest around you,
then they are not all there with you emotionally. It is human
nature to need convincing that we can really trust someone
totally before fully committing to them emotionally. This
does not come easily and will take time, especially if there
have been past experiences of failed trust. You need to be
patient and give them time to get to this place.

29. *In your opinion, what is the best way for us to communicate respectfully with each other?*

Different things make people feel disrespected - it can then lead to anger and resentment in a relationship. Knowing how a person expects to be addressed and communicated with can reduce the occasions when disrespect is perceived. Some people forget to show respect in a relationship after a while so some principles need to be agreed on how each person wants and expects to be spoken to and treated.

30. *Are you fully confident that I am the person you should be marrying?*

In the period leading to marriage, you must both feel at peace about the relationship's impending transition into a long-term marriage. It is one thing to be feeling anxious about the upcoming big day itself, but it's quite another thing if your anxiety comes from concerns about the rightness of your choice of person you are about to marry. For either of you to be feeling pangs of doubt at this stage, it might call for re-thinking of the decision to get married despite how far advanced the wedding plans are – extended time can settle some of these. Try to get to the bottom of the source of your negative feelings, it might be your sixth sense, instinct or God's Spirit in you (for those who are Christians), trying to tell you something. It is well worth finding this out as it could save you years of misery in a wrongly contracted marriage.

31. *Do you feel we both want the same things out of life?*

An excellent yet indirect question to help ascertain if you both have similar expectations out of the marital journey you are about to embark on. Not that your expectations are required to be the same, but it may be a concern if they are heading in completely opposite directions.

32. *(Question to the woman): To what extent are you willing to accept that there will be occasions when I will need to make certain unilateral decisions on behalf of both of us?*

This is NOT chauvinism but in a relationship of two, someone needs to be recognized as the leader, which in many instances turns out to be the man. In this capacity, it is usually expected that he will need to make decisions most times for both persons in the marriage. For leadership to be effective, it requires an enormous amount of trust on the part of the woman. If the woman has any reservations whatsoever about the man's ability to lead, then serious discussions will have to take place to arrive at what is acceptable to both parties.

33. *(Question to the man): To what extent can I trust you to be fair when making decisions on my behalf?*

This is the woman's perspective on how much she can trust her partner to make decisions on her behalf where there has been no consultation first. Fairness and a sound knowledge of her partner's ability to take her interest into consideration at all times are essential for her to support his decision making.

34. *(Question to the man): To what extent will you be willing to allow your spouse to make certain decisions on your behalf?*

It is often misconstrued that being a leader does not allow a husband to let his wife exercise her leadership potential too. The truth is, in the areas of her strengths (and his weaknesses), she is better placed to lead and, doing so does not in any way diminish his status as a leader.

35. *What are your main reasons for wanting to get married?*

People marry for various reasons and one of the most common ones cited is – companionship. This is the reason why the question asks for more than one reason. Apart from companionship, what are the other reasons? Look out for reasons that are long-term in nature because these reflect a willingness to spend their life with you.

36. *How do you cope with sexual temptations?*

After marriage neither party immediately becomes blind to the charms of the opposite sex, so a strategy needs to be developed to deal with sexual temptations when they come. Knowing that your partner has considered the reality of this, even if they have not perfected a strategy as yet, can bring some sense of relief. Perhaps, together, you can work out strategies to include ways in which you can help each other minimize the risk of falling prey to sexual temptation. This could be particularly useful if you have to be apart for any length of time.

37. Have you taken the time to understand the sexual anatomy of a man OR a woman?

Both need to be studied since people need to understand how their own bodies work as well as that of their partner. Without this knowledge, how do you expect to manage what you do not understand? The least you can do is try to understand that your partner is the most marvellous as well as complex creation in the entire universe. And when it comes to intimacy, ignorance is not bliss. You need to know how the body functions sexually in order to make your attempts at intimacy more meaningful and fulfilling.

38. Do you find me sexually attractive and, if so, under what circumstances is that attraction at its highest?

This is one of the few questions in this book that I'll allow you to let your imagination run wild in terms of why you think you need as an answer to it. All the best and am sure you will enjoy it.

39. *What positive things about me make up for the negative gaps in you?*

I personally love this one because it is one of the best reasons for wanting someone in your life.. The saying that "the two shall become one" reflects the concept of one person's negatives fitting into the other person's positives. When this happens, they work wonderfully together as one functioning unit. So, before you actually ask this question, find out what your biggest minuses and pluses are, so you can see how you fit together.

40. *How do you describe me to your friends?*

If your partner never talks about you to their friends this should send up a warning signal. It may not always be that they are ashamed of you. Maybe they wish to hide you for some other reason- good or bad. For example, they might be treading cautiously, wanting to make sure the relationship has a good chance of working before telling others about it. If the practice of not mentioning you to their friends persists after a while, the matter needs to be raised and discussed.

41. *What are some of the things that you thought about me when we first met that you do not think about me anymore?*

If your partner is getting to know you better, then some of the notions they had about you during the early moments of being attracted to you will be either confirmed or modified as they get to know you better.

42. *Do you believe that developing intimacy during marriage is a natural occurrence or it requires work?*

Intimacy is not only about having sex but involves really getting to know the person you have married very well. In this case, it takes time and deliberate effort on the part of both persons. From the sexual perspective, some persons believe that it is the husband's job to be romantic and then the wife will respond. Marriage is a partnership and both parties have a responsibility to keep the SPARK going – ensuring that each other's needs are met. Sometimes this requires you to overlook the fact that you are not at your best, yet make the effort to meet your partner's needs. This calls for commitment and willingness to put the other person's needs before yours. So, does your partner think intimacy occurs naturally or that it demands work and are you both willing to invest the energy it requires?

43. *Knowing me as I am and if nothing more were to change about me, would you still find it worth spending the rest of your life with me?*

Tell your partner this is the one question you want them to spend a week thinking about before answering. Insist on it and assure them that you will not be angry for being told the truth. This is a game-changer question because many people go into marriage secretly hoping that something about their partner will eventually change. The big question is- what happens if the change does not take place? Truth be told, it rarely ever does.

7

Establishing Your Own Family

This is where it all culminates. The diary of questions in this section will help you both appreciate each other's views, expectations, philosophies and beliefs on what constitutes a family and how it ought to be run. This is where you each have taken your individual family experiences, spiritual and social interactions, personal philosophies and other interactions to independently arrive at what you want in your own unique family. You both may not have built a family before but nonetheless, you will begin to see what it means to each of you, to have their own family. It certainly is not exhaustive, just like the other sections, but at least it will be a draft picture of building a family with your partner – one worth holding on to, until a real family unfolds.

1. *Do you want to have any children and how many?*

    The natural tendency is to assume that anyone who marries wants to have children - it is not necessarily true, so it needs to be asked. Having crossed that hurdle, then there is the issue of how many – a very important question for the woman's benefit since she will have to bear them.

2. *Where would you like to raise your children?*

    Where parents choose to live will definitely impact their children's development and future lives. So it is important to consider this when choosing a place to live. Some places are more child-friendly than others even within a particular country. So, it is not enough just to know where one wants to live but consideration should be given to the place deemed best suited to provide the best advantages for raising your children.

3. *How soon after marriage do you want to start having children?*

    This is a personal choice you and your partner are going to have to make and there really is no wrong or right answer. What I can say to you however, is that it is good to spend some time knowing each other and creating some good memories before you start having children because once children arrive, they take over your lives completely. So if you have no special memories of just the two of you to cherish during that temporary "takeover" period, you can end up feeling trapped and unfulfilled.

4. *How do you plan for us to care for our children if we are both working?*

These are hard questions. The quality of the care that you provide your children during their most formative and teachable ages are primarily what will determine how they turn out. Will a care giver be employed? Can family help? Will they go to day care or will one parent stay home? The last decision is likely to be based on the belief and the well-established fact that parents are the best ones to provide this kind of care in the early years, followed by family and then outsiders. If this is the case, then who should stay home with the children if that's the option agreed? Several factors will need to be considered and there are no easy answers. But if your children are important to you, then these issues must be discussed and a decision reached before the children show up.

5. *Should we both continue working while having babies and if not, what is the alternative?*

Marriage is serious business and requires proper planning. You need to wrestle with these questions and come up with the best solutions for the good of everyone involved. This question is proof of the type of hard issues you must grapple with and which require you to exercise your creative and critical thinking skills to produce workable solutions. The immediate tendency is to see how other people have done it and simply follow their example – but remember your family and its circumstances are unique and so too is the direction of your family's destiny.

6. *What would you do if we find out after marriage that we are unable to have children?*
This daunting possibility, although you might consider it remote, needs to be raised. Both partners must consider how important it is to have children and what you would do, if this doesn't materialize.

7. *What would be your family's reaction to our inability to have children?*
As insensitive as it may sound, the truth still remains that in certain cultures, childbearing is very important and to fail at it, brings a negative reaction and sometimes outright castigation of some sort. If by any chance, you or your partner comes from any of those cultures, this is a vital question to ask as well a plan on how to deal with it.

8. *Would you ever consider adopting a child?*
The question may arise within the context of infertility as well as from the view of it being a social good. It is a good question to ask considering that adoption is viewed differ-

ently by different people. Here is the chance to talk about it, even if it has only been remotely contemplated.

9. *What's your view on IVF for couples having difficulties conceiving naturally?*

This might be a decision you both have to make later in marriage and it usually raises religious and moral issues. There may at some point, be a need to settle the question if it is the child that matters or the process by which the child comes into existence. There are no easy answers here, but at least, this question can start you both thinking of embracing the option or finding others.

10. *What would you do if we had a disabled child?*

It is easy for people to say that whatever life throws at you is a blessing in disguise until life actually throws them bricks and they must now decide whether to use them to build walls or houses. This is not about life being fair, but about you being ready to deal with realities when they occur. It is good to give some consideration to these things before they happen albeit it is not my wish that it does – nevertheless, my wishes cannot play God.

11. What do you believe should be the roles of a father and mother?

For you and your partner, there is a high probability that the biggest concept of fatherhood or motherhood you know is one you learnt from your own parents or guardians – and they are definitely different. What you have known until now, may not necessarily be the best approach to raising your own family. What you also want to avoid is to walk into marriage with a certain understanding of these roles only to be met by one substantively different viewpoint from your partner – one that you were not mentally ready to embrace.

12. What do you consider as the best way to parenting our children?

Parenting duties do not need to be fixed. They are likely to have changed during the centuries and in today's society, these roles are even more fluid. It requires much flexibility, insight and wisdom to successfully raise children in our contemporary society. This question should generate a good discussion and should not be about who is right or wrong, but about what is likely to produce the best results, given the world we live in and its fast paced nature..

13. *What is it about your wider family would you like to bring into our own family?*

No matter how dysfunctional your partner's family may have been, there are still some good things from it that could be of value to the family you are about to establish. Talk about these and begin to consider some of the ways you can incorporate them into your family. It may even be rewarding to your partner to note that the family they were hewn from is acknowledged as having some value worth emulating.

14. *Do you have valuable childhood experiences you'd like your own children to have?*

This is moving away from the general family to the specific area of childhood. I still carry some exceptional memories of my growing up and indeed they have contributed so much to my life that I think I would be cheating my children if I denied them these same experiences. You might be pleasantly surprised that the areas in which your childhood experiences weren't great may turn out to be the areas in which your partner's were good and as a unified team, you could formulate overall rewarding experiences for your children.

15. *Are there any childhood experiences that you would not want your own children to have?*

If there were unpleasant experiences your partner had in childhood that have lingered in their memory till date, it tells you the depth to which they were mentally imprinted. Knowing this can be very helpful in preventing your children from having to be marred with similar negative lifetime experiences if not guided.

16. *How do you plan for us to manage our finances once we get married?*

This is one of those subjects that must be talked about at great length to establish a mutually accepted approach to the way money will be handled as a family. There is no way it should be avoided and simple answers will not be enough – the details must be spelled out. Issues regarding money have been known to cause endless conflict in marriages and sometimes ultimately lead to their dissolution. This calls for in-depth discussion, and my advice to you - talk about absolutely everything related to money. It is that important.

17. *What are your long-term plans for our family's investments?*

Wise forward planning of finances is important because the cost for raising a family is not only immediate but long-term. It is also crucial to understand your partner's perspectives on preparing for life's contingencies. It is in your own interest and peace of mind to create some form of security for your family's financial future with or without your partner's input.

18. What are some of the practical ways we should consider raising our children to be financially sound?

I suppose this is not the way most people would think about it. The usual thinking is to raise kids, give them a good education and they have a good chance of growing up to be financially sound in a good job or business. But the truth is children need to be taught financial literacy that will aid in their own wealth creation. They can be taught about savings, entrepreneurship and spending within their means, among other things. These sound financial habits are likely to continue into their adult lives.

19. What 5 absolute financial boundaries will you expert everyone to adhere to in our family?

Every family needs boundaries where its finances are concerned and parents are expected to set the guidelines for this. I do not want to sound too prescriptive, but if the adults in the family follow these set rules themselves, children will follow suit.

20. How do you plan to go about disciplining our children ?

It is always a good idea to arrive at a mutual agreement as to how to discipline your children, then resolving to implement it jointly, when the time comes. We know all too well the situation where one parent says no and the child goes to the other parent, hoping for a different response. A united front in this case is your best approach when enforcing discipline because it not only prevents the children from playing one parent against the other – it also depicts consistency in parenting.

21. What was your relationship like with your parent of the opposite sex?

This is likely to form the foundation of your partner's understanding of how a man or woman functions as parent in a marriage. It can explain some of your partner's attitudes and behaviour as well as what they expect of you.

22. What is the biggest lesson on parenting you've learned from your own parents?

People tend to parent the way they were parented, therefore, it is good to know which aspects of their parents' style they wish to emulate and those they wish to avoid. You might not agree with all that is said, so raising this question will give you a chance to air you opinion and arrive at some common ground for parenting.

23. Are there any special traditions you would like to establish in your own family?

Family traditions are important as a means of bonding and creating special memories that will last a lifetime whether they are practised daily, weekly, monthly or yearly. It could be something as simple as always eating dinner together or the way you celebrate Christmas. Beside the closeness these occasions create, they also give the family something pleasurable to anticipate.

24. What is your view on a parent's role in guiding children into what careers they choose?

The days are over when parents unilaterally decided what careers their children grew into. Although this is the reality, there is still need for parental guidance which should be based, in large part, on what parents observe are the peculiar abilities and talents of the child. Knowing this should assist parents in guiding children along the path that will allow them to make maximum use of their special strengths and abilities.

25. To what extent do you want extended families on both sides to be a part of our family life?

In answering this question, a lot is going to be influenced by the impact you or your partner's extended family each had on you individually. You just need to make sure it does not get in the way of what might be best for your own children. It is worthwhile for each of you to actually engage in a self-audit to determine if your own personal experiences with extended families should automatically be repeated for your own children.

26. *Within marriage, how much need do you see for individual privacy?*

The marital truth of two people becoming one, is not agreeable to everybody in its entirety. For some, it still doesn't mean all of a person's individual privacy be surrendered – including their need for personal space. As to the extent, frequency, timing and boundaries of any such individual privacy, it is totally up to you two to decide. This could be generating much debate, but it is an essential one so as not to give the other party a sense of being smothered or losing their individuality.

27. *Is it possible to treat all our children equally or would there always be a favourite?*

There is always the chance that this will inevitably happen and as parents, there is no need beating yourself about it – you will always feel more inclined towards one of your children than the rest. Denying that such a phenomenon exists is an even greater danger. What you should bear in mind, is to try as much as possible not to make it evident before the other children. In reality, you don't need to make an effort to be endeared to your favourite child – it's the other(s) you have to make a conscious effort to assure they are equal.

28. *What habits as a child had a negative impact on you that you would like to prevent your children from developing?*

Well, this is assuming that you or your partner have been able to overcome those habits and have learnt from it and want to impart these lessons to your children. The feel-good nature of this question is that at least one of you would have experienced the related habits first-hand and are therefore better placed to gauge what its likely impact on your off-springs are likely to be.

29. *What behaviours would you discourage exhibiting before your children?*

Indeed, there are some acts between you and your partner that as much as possible should be restricted from the view of your children. Some people, for example, feel it is alright for parents to argue in front of the children because it is one of the realities of life and they need to embrace it. But this is just one side of the equation. The other side of it is that you may be causing psychological damage to that child who does not yet understand or fully grasp what is going on and may misinterpret it. Find out if there are other things that your partner would not want displayed before children.

30. Would you defend your spouse before your family even if they were wrong?

If you have the opportunity to ask this question, follow up with a "why?" This will certainly be an interesting topic. What I will say, however, is that – how you deal with your partner in front of members of your larger family will to a large extent determine how your family deals with your partner.

31. How do you intend to honour work commitments and still make time for your family?

Now, this is a question to test your partner's understanding of the need to strike a balance between commitment to family and the obligations to work. Too often family time is sacrificed on the altar of work, and this applies to both of you. Some firm guidelines must be worked out to safeguard against this happening.

32. What language(s) should be spoken at home?

This question is usually relevant to couples with different mother tongues. Remember, that children have the extraordinary ability to learn multiple languages simultaneously and that research shows that doing this actually improves some of their brain functions.

33. *What are the most important values you believe we should teach our children?*

Every family tends to have a set of core values that they try to pass on to generations – it is these values that differentiate one family from another.. Whether it is the virtue of hard work and honesty, or loyalty to god and country or such, they are what we believe is intrinsically good for the individual and the wider society. I would recommend two - gratitude and loyalty – that should be on your list.

34. *If for any reason I was suddenly unable to support our family financially in the manner I usually would, how would you handle it?*

Life is filled with uncertainties and while we cannot predict them all, it is useful to anticipate some of the likely impacts and reactions some events could cause. Asking this question might encourage your partner to consider something they might have given little thought to previously. This, is reality.

35. *If we have an unresolved problem in our marriage, whom would you prefer me to first consult about it?*

Some people would immediately say nobody, but there comes a time when you need to talk to someone and you need to know your partner's preference so they will not be too offended to discover that you have spoken to someone about the matter. You might ask them who would they prefer you to consult and in what order of priority from a list of persons such as a church leader, marriage counsellor, parents or any family member, siblings and any other person you think they might consider appropriate. Their choice of persons can say a lot about their allegiances as well as their priorities in terms of values. For example, if they choose someone from the church, it might be indicative of the importance they place on spiritual things.

36. *After childbirth or a serious illness, it may be useful to have an extra helping hand. If the only persons available were my father, mother, siblings, or my best friend – who would you prefer helps?*

It does not necessarily mean when the time comes, the choices will remain the same, but at least you will know ahead of time who the top two preferences are likely to be. It may well turn out your partner may have difficulty accepting anyone from your side of the family. Don't attack the issue, find out why.

37. *Do you consider family holidays essential?*

Culture plays a big part in this. But beyond that, my personal argument has always been – even God rested after creating the world and indeed he commands holidays in the Bible. In any case, holiday's bring new life to whole families and provide refreshing opportunities to rekindle family bonds and create new memories. I suspect the first concern for people about family holidays is that – they can be expensive. Truth is, they might not be if you take time to plan them well, even in-country holidays can still be very refreshing. None of this however is relevant if you both do not agree that holidays are essential for maintaining good family bonds.

38. What types of education do you consider crucial (formal and/or informal) to give our children and how will they receive it and at what stages?

I think a good balance is for children to have formal and informal education. Many people rely on formal education, but don't be fooled, there are still an awful lot of useful life-skills to learn from informal education opportunities, if the programmes are well planned. An important thing to realize as aspiring parents is that you may not have absolutely ALL the insight needed to raise a perfect child – it may be useful to identify some important people in your spheres, what life-skills they can impact your children with that you and your partner don't currently possess and arranging the best way to have it delivered.

39. When babies come along, who will take prime responsibility for looking after them?

Looking after children, especially babies, requires work and lots of it - so it merits a lengthy discussion. In my opinion, this should be a shared task, and I always suggest it is based on each person's individual strengths. For example, my personal body clock is so used to me staying up late nights to work – thus me taking the night shifts for our new born children was a breeze in the park and it allowed my wife to catch her breath even if for a few hours.

40. As a family, how should we prepare for financial emergencies that may arise in the future?

It is not what many like to talk about but it provides some peace of mind, knowing that in an emergency, financial pressures can be mitigated. Believe me, dealing with the stress of any emergency can be almost overwhelming on its own, let alone combining it with financial pressures. Having a good insurance plan in times of emergency goes a long way to reduce the burden.

41. How would you react if any of your children told you that they were Lesbian or Gay?

No matter how in tune you are with the changes in the world, it might still be a bit of a surprise if your child announces that they are gay. Being prepared ahead of time for such an eventuality will certainly help to lessen the shock it might cause you both. The question may even jolt the need to face up to the reality that being proactive and carrying out practical steps to prevent it happening is a more reassuring approach to confronting this, as opposed to simply assuming it won't happen.

42. *How would you react if your daughter got pregnant while unmarried; of if your son put a girl he is not married to, in the family way?*

Again, as in the question above, you and your partner obviously cannot shield your children from interacting with the world, society and especially the opposite sex. But again, realizing that unwed pregnancies do take place might make you do some contingency planning as well as change some of the ways you plan to raise your children.

43. *How do you plan to counteract the negative moral influences of society on our children?*

Children are exposed every day to the various negative influences at school, through the media and by their encounter with other people holding different values. It becomes quite a challenge for parents to instil positive values in the face of all this, but it must be done. A deliberate effort has to be made to ensure that family values and traditions are transmitted to the young to counteract the less than desirable influences from the society. This calls for the consideration of specific strategies for confronting the situation.

44. Do you see your home as a sanctuary of peace and quiet or as an open space to receive, entertain and enjoy your relationship with family and friends?

This question is likely to help both you and your partner make the family home the best place you will each want to be in. Some persons prefer peace and quiet with occasional friendly visits, others like the idea of an open house. Very often it calls for a compromise of one sort or the other. As much as possible, each should try to lessen the occasions when you make your homes unwelcoming to your spouse. Bearing that in mind, it is also important to keep in mind that inasmuch as you may want your home to be a sanctuary of peace – your family cannot survive in isolation and as such, your home needs to be open to people from time to time.

In Conclusion

Finally then, remember human beings evolve and develop new perspectives on life over time. This means some of the answers given today might not be relevant in the future, therefore, it is important to ask some of these same questions after a few years of being married. This will give you an opportunity to find out what has changed and what you might need to adjust.

It is my sincerest hope that whatever mix of conversations, doubts, controversies, confirmations, hopes and assurances are generated from the questions in this book, it will help you make the best decisions regarding marriage. I pray it all works for your good.

Appendix of Bible Scriptures

1 Corinthians 7:1-40
1 Corinthians 13:4-7
Ephesians 5:22-33
Genesis 2:24
Proverbs 18:22
Hebrews 13:4
Ephesians 5:25-33
Proverbs 21:9
Proverbs 19:14
Matthew 19:2-9
1 Corinthians 7:39
1 Corinthians 13:4-10
Malachi 2:13-16
2 Corinthians 6:14
Ephesians 5:31
Ephesians 5:25
Ephesians 5:33
Matthew 5:32
Psalm 85:10
1 Corinthians 7:12-15
1 Peter 3:1-11
1 Corinthians 13:4-8
1 Corinthians 11:11
Matthew 19:9
1 Peter 3:1
Hebrews 13:1-25
Hosea 2:19
1 Corinthians 11:12
Isaiah 62:5
Proverbs 21:19
Ephesians 3:14-21
Galatians 2:20
Matthew 22:30

1 Corinthians 6:16
Luke 16:18
Colossians 3:18
Matthew 12:25
1 Timothy 3:12
Matthew 19:29
Leviticus 21:7
Romans 7:3
Matthew 18:20
Proverbs 25:24
1 Peter 3:1-13
Genesis 2:23
Mark 10:2-12
Psalm 37:4
Ecclesiastes 3:11
Mark 10:6-9
1 Corinthians 13:4-13
1 Timothy 5:14
Genesis 2:18
1 Corinthians 13:4
Ecclesiastes 4:9-12
Mark 12:25
Genesis 2:1-25
Mark 10:11
1 Timothy 4:3
1 Corinthians 7:8
Romans 7:1-6
Leviticus 20:14
Genesis 28:2
Luke 1:27
Philippians 4:13
Matthew 1:18
Genesis 1:27

Jeremiah 2:32
Genesis 29:15-30
1 Corinthians 7:7
Matthew 19:3-9
Matthew 19:3
Matthew 5:31
Leviticus 20:19-21
Genesis 38:8
Genesis 20:3
Revelation 1:1-20
Galatians 5:13
Hosea 1:2
Genesis 2:20-24
Song of Solomon 2:14
Esther 2:2-4
1 Corinthians 9:5
Malachi 2:11
Exodus 34:16
Genesis 20:9-16
Mark 10:12
1 Timothy 3:2
1 Corinthians 13:4-6
Romans 7:1-3
Jeremiah 29:6
1 Corinthians 7:24-40
1 John 4:7
1 Corinthians 13:1-13
Exodus 22:16
Hosea 2:20
1 Corinthians 7:1-6
Ephesians 5:30-32
Genesis 2:22-25
Romans 7:2
Ezekiel 16:8

Author's other works

Title:	Is This Why Africa Is? (E-book & Paperback)
Description:	I ask all the questions about Africa that nobody else will. Deep, profound questions
Availability:	Amazon & Kindle
Link to View:	http://goo.gl/ecRMig

Title:	Where Did God Hide His Diamonds? (E-book & Paperback)
Description:	Discovering what exactly God has hidden in you, finding it & prospering freely from it
Availability:	Amazon & Kindle
Link to View:	http://goo.gl/ecRMig

Title:	Doing Business with God (E-book & Paperback)
Description:	60 shocking biblical principles for extraordinary leadership, business and politics.
Availability:	Amazon & Kindle
Link to View:	http://goo.gl/ecRMig

Title:	Midnight Philosophies (E-book & Paperback)
Description:	My Deep thoughts, Philosophies, Reflections – Whispers of my mind.
Availability:	Amazon & Kindle
Link to View:	http://goo.gl/ecRMig

Title:	This Godly Child of Mine (E-book & Paperback)
Description:	A revelatory book on how to raise godly children in a perverse and lawless world
Availability:	Amazon & Kindle
Link to View:	http://goo.gl/ecRMig

Title:	The Deputy Minister for Corruption (E-book & Paperback)
Description:	A Novel
Availability:	Amazon & Kindle
Link to View:	http://goo.gl/ecRMig

Title:	A Dove in the Storm (E-book & Paperback)
Description:	A Novel
Availability:	Amazon & Kindle
Link to View:	http://goo.gl/ecRMig

Title:	100% JOB INTERVIEW SUCCESS (E-book & Paperback)
Description:	A simple, straightforward guide to passing every job interview you attend.
Availability:	Amazon & Kindle
Link to View:	http://goo.gl/ecRMig

Title:	Bible-by-Heart (Mobile App)
Description:	A simple but effective App to help anyone memorize 500 Bible verses in a year.
Availability:	iTunes & Google Play Stores

Link to View: http://goo.gl/T3UdPN (i-Tunes)

Link to View: http://goo.gl/ljnECR (Android)

Title: Holy Rat (Mobile Game)

Description: An exciting Christian mobile game that unwittingly

gets you addicted to the word.

Availability: iTunes & Google Play Stores

Link to View: http://goo.gl/bygjBi (i-Tunes)

Link to View: http://goo.gl/F18RM0 (Android)

ABOUT THE AUTHOR

Marricke Kofi Gane, is a gifted African Author, Philosopher, Public Speaker, Coach and Educationist. His writings carry real depth, are highly motivating yet challenging every status quo. He displays dexterity of mind and refined humour where appropriate. He is never shy in some of his works, to show a strong balance between his Christian roots and the reality of living in today's world.

Discover for yourself, all that his writings stand for - to dare, to motivate, to impact!! For more on him, visit www.marrickekofigane.com

Dear Reader,

Thank you for reading this book. I am hopeful that the information provided in it has given you some new learning, challenged you, or provided some answers and inspiration.

I respectfully ask your indulgence in 2 simple ways:

1. Whatever positive action(s) this book has inspired you to take, DO IT NOW. Not later.

2. Help other potential readers who without you, may never read this book by simply following the link below to leave a review. It only takes 3 minutes, but it could be a lifetime blessing for someone out there.

    http://goo.gl/v03bu2 0

Thank you once again for everything

Marricke Kofi GANE

Thurs Dec 6th   6:30

Cindi Hartman 706 338 0404

40-50   tables?

plastic plates , forks, glasses

drinks   bucket w/ ice

wine →

ice

water   tea

☐ heat pads for dishes

parking sign

trash

music

lights decorations